DK SMITHSONIAN ☀

QUIZ
YOURSELF
CLEVER!
ROCKS &
MINERALS

Produced for DK by Just Content Limited
10A Little Square, Braintree, Essex, CM7 1UT

Editorial Just Content Limited
Design PDQ Digital Media Solutions, Bungay, UK

Senior editor Shaila Brown
US editor Michael Nolan
Senior art editor Jacqui Swan
Managing editor Rachel Fox
Managing art editor Owen Peyton Jones
Production editor Gillian Reid
Production controller Laura Andrews
Jacket designer Vidushi Chaudhry
DTP designer Deepak Mittal
Senior jackets coordinator Priyanka Sharma Saddi
Jacket design development manager Sophia MTT
Publisher Andrew Macintyre
Associate publishing director Liz Wheeler
Art director Karen Self
Publishing director Jonathan Metcalf

First American Edition, 2024
Published in the United States by DK Publishing,
a division of Penguin Random House LLC
1745 Broadway, 20th Floor, New York, NY 10019

A catalog record for this book is available from
the Library of Congress.
ISBN: 978-0-5938-4151-8

DK books are available at special discounts when purchased in bulk
for sales promotions, premiums, fund-raising, or educational use.
For details, contact: DK Publishing Special Markets, 1745 Broadway,
20th Floor, New York, NY 10019 or SpecialSales@dk.com

Printed and bound in China

www.dk.com

The name of the Smithsonian Institution and the sunburst logo
are registered trademarks of the Smithsonian Institution.
For more information, please visit www.si.edu

Smithsonian

Contents

How to use this book

Quizzes are one of the best ways to learn new facts and test your knowledge. You can do the quizzes by yourself, with a friend, or in teams.

How to play
Try answering the questions on the right-hand page. You'll find all the answers on the next page. How many questions did you get right? If you want to increase your scores and boost your brain power, reread the profile and test yourself again! If you're playing with friends, you'll need pen and paper to write down the answers. Whoever gets the most correct answers wins!

A description of the rock or mineral at the top of the page provides a clue.

These are the questions about the rock or mineral.

Rich blue-green

What mineral is this?

This mineral is found all over the **world**. True or false?

The name of this mineral is derived from which two Greek words?

Does this mineral have a **dull** appearance?

Is it prized as a **gemstone**?

Who **first** used the name of this mineral in 315 BCE?

Orthorhombic
Silicates

203

The name of the mineral or rock group, and for minerals also the crystal system group (the maximum symmetry of their faces), appears at the bottom of the page to help you guess the rock or mineral's identity.

The common name is revealed on the next page.

Chrysocolla

The term chrysocolla was first used by the Greek philosopher Theophrastus in 315 BCE to refer to various materials used in soldering gold. The name is derived from two Greek words: *chrysos*, which means "gold," and *kolla*, which means "glue."

The fact box provides some of the answers.

Location Worldwide
Color Blue, blue-green
Luster Glassy to earthy
Hardness 2-4
Streak Pale blue, tan, gray

This bird resting on a cluster of berries has been carved from chrysocolla.

Further details about the rock or mineral are given, such as different varieties, facts about its history, and interesting examples of how it is used.

Rich blue-green chrysocolla, such as the stone in this bracelet, is highly prized as a gemstone.

Theophrastus was the first scholar to attempt a systematic classification of gems and minerals.

204

There are fun facts on each rock or mineral profile, which also provide answers to some of the questions.

What's in the fact box

Rocks

Type
The type of rock; for example, igneous, sedimentary, or metamorphic.

Grain size
Geologists can identify rocks by their grain size.

The grains of igneous rocks below ground are large, as they have enough time to grow. When magma erupts from volcanoes, the lava cools down rapidly. This gives little time for grains to develop.

Grains in metamorphic rocks grow slowly. Large grains indicate that the rock was formed under high pressure and heat. Rocks that form under lower pressure and heat have smaller grains.

The grains in sedimentary rocks are of different sizes and textures.

Major minerals / Minor minerals
Rocks consist of minerals—usually several of them. The major minerals are the main components of the rock; the minor minerals are the lesser components of the rock.

Color
Color is used to tell different varieites of a rock apart, and it can also provide information on the composition of the rock.

Minerals

Location
Gems are found worldwide, but some areas are exceptionally rich sources. Myanmar, for example, contributes a huge amount of the world's ruby supply, while Madagascar is richest in sapphires.

Color
In gems, color is caused when light is absorbed within the crystal or refracted—changing direction as it passes through the gem. White light is composed of many colors; when one or more of those colors is absorbed, the remaining light emerging from the gem is colored.

Luster
Luster is the way a mineral reflects light. There are a number of terms to describe this—waxy, metallic, earthy, adamantine, resinous, pitchy, dull, greasy, oily, pearly, silky, velvety, or glassy (vitreous).

Hardness
One of the easiest tests is to find a mineral's hardness. This is measured on the Mohs scale—a relative scale, from 1–10, tested by scratching the mineral, or by using it to scratch something else.

Streak
A mineral may not always appear the same color. It may have been altered by weathering, for example. So, geologists carry a hard ceramic scratch plate and test a mineral's streak, which does not vary.

Our rocky planet

Earth is a rocky ball, with thick molten rock near its center. Only a thin surface shell of the planet is solid. This crust is made of rocky minerals—mainly combinations of silicon and oxygen called silicates—and is up to 31 miles (50 km) thick. Heat from inside the planet keeps the crust moving.

Inner core is 745 miles (1,200 km) thick

Outer core is 1,430 miles (2,300 km) thick

Mantle is 1,800 miles (2,900 km) thick

Land surface is made of continental crust

Continental crust is up to 31 miles (50 km) thick

How Earth formed

The planets of the Solar System formed around the same time, about 4.6 billion years ago, from the cloud of dusty rubble orbiting the Sun. Over millions of years, small clumps of this debris grew larger and were pulled into spheres by the force of their own gravity. As the sphere grew, it attracted more and more debris, accelerating the growth of our planet.

Earth cooled to become a rocky planet, with oceans, continents, and an atmosphere.

This artwork shows a sequence of how Earth formed—from small fragments of rock and dust sticking together to a planet that has its own atmosphere.

The rock cycle

Many different types of rock have developed over billions of years through a variety of processes. These processes are linked in a never-ending cycle known as the rock cycle.

1. Wind, rain, and other processes weather rock, turning it into small particles of sand and clay that wash away in rain.

2. Sediment from rivers builds up on the seabed and, over millions of years, turns into sedimentary rock.

4. Very high temperatures melt rock. When the molten rock cools, it solidifies into igneous rock.

3. Pressure and heat in Earth's interior slowly change rock, turning it into metamorphic rock.

Rocks

A rock is a naturally occurring material consisting of one or more minerals, although a few rocks are made of other substances. For example, coal is made of decayed vegetation.

Tourmaline crystal

Quartz

Tourmaline pegmatite

Pegmatite is an igneous rock that forms during the final stage of magma's crystallization.

Types of rock

Scientists can classify almost all rocks into one of three main types, depending on how the rocks form. The types are known as igneous rock, sedimentary rock, and metamorphic rock. About 90 percent of the rock in Earth's crust is igneous.

Granite

Igneous rocks
These are formed from magma (molten rock) that has either solidified underground, creating intrusive rocks such as granite, or has flowed onto the land or sea bed, forming extrusive rocks such as basalt.

Sedimentary rocks
Sand, mud, and even the remains of living organisms can turn into rock. These sediments settle on the seafloor, building up in layers. Water seeping through the layers deposits minerals that glue the sediment particles together. Shale and sandstone form this way.

Sandstone

Marble

Metamorphic
Deep underground, rock can be subjected to intense heat and pressure. These forces can cause minerals to recrystallize. The result is a hard, crystalline type of rock called metamorphic rock, which frequently has stripy patterns. Examples include marble and slate.

Rocks in the landscape

Most of Earth's rocks are hidden beneath the surface, but in some places they are visible in the landscape. The way in which a rock is made can affect what it looks like. Lava can harden into amazing shapes as it cools, and sedimentary rock created by different layers of sediment may have beautiful bands of color within it.

Devil's Tower, Wyoming
This giant structure of phonolite, an igneous rock, formed when a volcano erupted and the magma cooled and solidified to form underground columns. Over millions of years, its surrounding layers weathered away, leaving the columns exposed.

Amitsoq gneiss rock, Greenland
So far, the oldest rocks found on Earth's surface are metamorphic gneisses. The Amitsoq gneiss rock outcrop, on the western fringe of Greenland, dates back 3.8 billion years and shows the banded structure typical of gneiss.

The Grand Canyon, Arizona
One of the deepest river gorges in the world, the Grand Canyon was created by the colossal forces that build mountains. The result is a spectacular canyon, displaying layers of sedimentary rock. The highest layers are the youngest, while the deepest are the oldest.

Rocks from outer space

Look up at the sky on a clear night and you may see a shooting star. More than 120 tons (110 tonnes) of dust and rocky fragments blaze in from space every day. Some space rocks called meteoroids enter Earth's atmosphere and burn up, creating a streak of light known as a meteor. The meteoroids that survive and land on the ground are called meteorites. These are of three types—iron, stony-iron, and stony meteorites.

The Hoba meteorite is the largest on Earth. The iron meteorite is thought to have landed about 80,000 years ago, and still lies at Hoba Farm, Namibia, where it was found in 1920.

Minerals

Minerals are the basic building blocks of solid Earth. All rocks are made out of tiny, mixed mineral grains. Each mineral has a definite chemical recipe, and can be identified by its crystal form (known as its habit), color, hardness, surface shine (luster), and the way in which it breaks.

A definite chemical composition and an ordered internal arrangement of atoms gives minerals the flat faces and sharp edges of crystals.

The rich purple color is due to traces of iron and radiation.

Amethyst

Minerals are naturally occurring solids. Some form solid crystals as molten liquid rock cools; others crystallize out of fluids loaded with dissolved minerals trickling through the rocks.

Gems

A gemstone, or gem, is a mineral that has been polished and shaped by a skilled craftsperson in order to enhance its beauty. The most highly prized gems are hard-wearing and rare. There are more than 5,000 known minerals on Earth, but fewer than 100 are used as gems.

Gems often look dull before they are cut and polished.

Different cuts bring out the beauty of a gem.

Uncut amethyst crystal

Gems are exceptionally beautiful crystals that are shaped and polished to enhance their appearance.

Oval mixed-cut amethyst

Organic gems

These are made from animal or plant materials. For instance, coral is formed from sea creatures, pearls develop in certain shellfish such as oysters, and amber is made of fossilized tree resin.

Violet coral

Pearl oyster

Amber

Crystal systems

Minerals have different crystal systems (crystal shapes). The shape of a crystal is determined by how its atoms are arranged. This determines the number of flat sides, sharp edges, and corners of a crystal. Crystals are sorted into six main groups, according to which 3-D pattern they fit.

Cubic
Crystals in this system are common and easily recognized. They have three axes at right angles, and shapes can be four- or eight-sided.

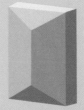

Orthorhombic
Crystals in this system are similar to the monoclinic system, but all three axes are at right angles. Habits are tabular and prismatic.

Tetragonal
Tetragonal crystals have three axes of symmetry, all at right angles, two of which are of equal length.

Trigonal and hexagonal
Both these systems are similar, with four axes of symmetry. Crystals are often six-sided with tops like a pyramid.

Monoclinic
The monoclinic system has crystals with three unequal axes of symmetry, only two at right angles. Tabular and prismatic shapes are common.

Triclinic
Triclinic crystals have the least symmetrical shape, because their three axes are unequal in length and are not at right angles.

Peridot

Carats
A carat is the standard measure of weight for precious stones and metals. One carat is equal to 0.007 oz (0.2 g). It is also used as a measure of the purity of gold—pure gold being 24 carats.

Classifying minerals

There are thousands of minerals on Earth, based on the chemicals they contain. While some minerals are abundant, others—including diamonds—are very rare and highly prized. Shown below are the major chemical groups, with an example of each.

Gold

Native elements
Most minerals are made of two or more chemical elements bonded together. A small handful, however, are not combined with anything else and are found in their natural, or native, state. Some of these minerals are highly valued precious metals.

Sphalerite

Sulfides
Among the most important metal ores in the world, sulfides are a group of commonly dark, dense minerals made of sulfur combined with metal. Sulfides do not usually make good gemstones because they are too soft.

Sapphire

Oxides
Many minerals contain oxygen, but oxide minerals are specifically those formed by one or more elements teamed with oxygen. Oxides are often stunning, and this group features some of the most gorgeous, glittering gemstones.

Sylvite

Halides
Halides are a group of sometimes brightly colored minerals that form when metallic elements combine with halogen elements. The halogens are fluorine, chlorine, bromine, and iodine.

Diaspore

Hydroxides

Hydroxide minerals are typically secondary minerals that form when water reacts with existing rocks and minerals. Other mineral groups can become hydrated when water molecules are incorporated into the crystal structure.

Smithsonite

Carbonates

The carbonates are a family of relatively soft minerals that are formed of metal elements, along with carbon and oxygen. Carbonates are abundant in sea water, and some sea creatures such as mollusks use carbonate minerals to build their shells.

Apatite

Phosphates

The phosphates are a family of minerals that contain phosphorus and oxygen. They are part of a large and varied group that includes the arsenates and vanadates. Bright colors are characteristic of this group of minerals.

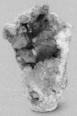
Celestine

Sulfate minerals

The sulfates, tungstates, chromates, and molybdates are minerals that show a similar chemical structure. Oxygen combines with sulfur, tungsten, chromium, and molybdenum respectively to form these minerals. The sulfates are the most common.

Olivine

Silicates

The silicates are the most common minerals on Earth. They are made up of silicon and oxygen, combined with other elements, mostly metals. These minerals are the main ingredients in sands and clays, and are found in almost all rocks.

Amber

Organic minerals

Organic minerals, or mineraloids, are often hard substances made by living things. Unlike minerals that have an ordered internal crystal arrangement, mineraloids may or may not have a regular crystal structure.

The quiz starts here...

Carving favorite

What **rock** is this?

Why is it good for **carving**?

Is it a **commonly** found rock?

How is it **formed**?

What famous **monument** in South Dakota is made from it?

Can you name one of the **major** minerals found in this rock?

Granite

Familiar as a mottled pink, white, grey, and black ornamental stone, granite is the most common rock type in Earth's continental crust. It forms by the cooling of magma deep below Earth's surface. Its strength and durability have made it a favorite stone for carving and building for at least 4,000 years.

Type Silica-rich, plutonic

Grain size $\frac{1}{16}$–$\frac{3}{16}$ in (2–5 mm), phenocrysts to 4 in (10 cm)

Major minerals Potassium feldspar, quartz, mica

Minor minerals Sodium plagioclase, hornblende

Color White, light gray, pink, red

This Bronze Age axe head is carved from granite.

Over time, granite breaks down to create much of the quartz sand on beaches.

Granite is ideal for making long-lasting sculptures. The heads of four American presidents were chiselled straight out of a granite cliff called Mount Rushmore in South Dakota.

Precious gems

Tourmalines are found in this rock. True or false?

Can you name one of the **minor** minerals found in this rock?

What **rock** is this?

What **colors** can it be?

Why is it useful in producing industrial **metals**?

Which gemstone mined from this rock looks like a **fruit**?

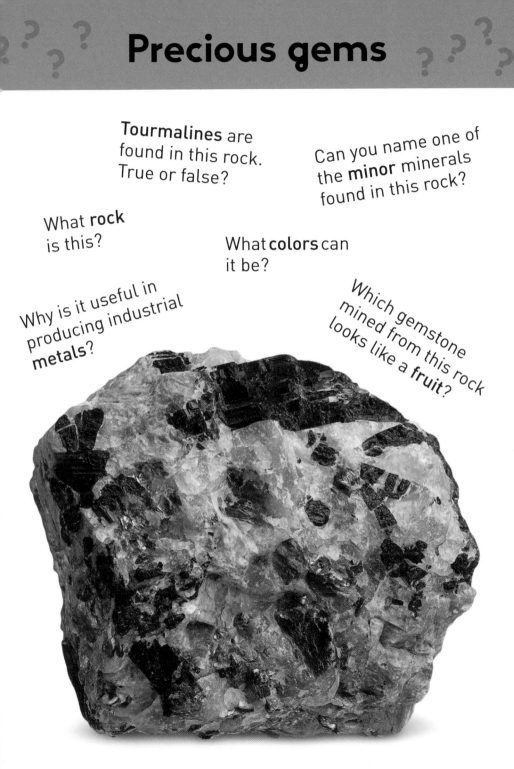

Pegmatite

Pegmatites are light-colored rocks and occur in small igneous bodies, such as veins and dykes, or sometimes as patches in larger masses of granite. Several gemstones—such as tourmaline group minerals, aquamarine, rock crystal, smoky quartz, rose quartz, and topaz—are mined from pegmatites.

Type Feldspar-rich, plutonic

Grain size ³⁄₁₆ in (5 mm) to many meters

Major minerals Quartz, feldspar, mica

Minor minerals Tourmaline, topaz

Color White, pink

Tourmaline crystals with a pink center and a green rim, or vice-versa, are called watermelon tourmaline, because their coloring is similar to the pink flesh and green rind of a watermelon.

Most topaz specimens are yellow and brown. Colorless or gray stones are also common, while pink and blue ones are rarer.

Some pegmatites contain minerals that are the source of industrial metals like tin.

Metal source

What **rock** is this?

It is mined for valuable metals such as **nickel**. True or false?

Is it always a **dark-colored** rock?

What is its **grain** size?

Why does it sometimes have a greenish **tinge**?

How does it **form**?

Gabbro

Gabbros occur as intrusions and as uplifted sections of oceanic crust. Some gabbros are mined for their nickel, chromium, and platinum. Those containing ilmenite and magnetite are mined for their iron or titanium. Pyroxene minerals give gabbros a greenish tinge.

Type Mafic, plutonic

Grain size $1/16$–$3/16$ in (2–5 mm)

Major minerals Calcium plagioclase feldspar, pyroxene, ilmenite

Minor minerals Olivine, magnetite

Color Dark gray to black

This gabbro has bands of light and dark minerals.

The top of oceanic crust is made of basalt. Deeper down, the rocks cool more slowly to make gabbro.

Gabbro is found in the Cuillins layered intrusion, in the rugged landscape of Scotland's Isle of Skye.

Salt-and-pepper rock

What **rock** is this?

How was it used in ancient **Egypt**?

It is always a **dark-colored** rock. True or false?

Is it a **tough** rock?

What is its **grain** size?

What other **name** is it called?

Diorite

A prized rock in ancient Egypt, diorite was used to build columns, figures, and sarcophagi (stone coffins), and for lining the chambers of some pyramids. This igneous rock consists of white plagioclase and dark hornblende in roughly equal proportions. Diorite is sometimes called black granite.

Type Intermediate silica content, plutonic

Grain size $1/16$–$3/16$ in (2–5 mm)

Major minerals Sodium plagioclase, hornblende

Minor minerals Biotite

Color Black or dark green mottled with gray or white

Diorite is called a "salt-and-pepper" rock due to its coloring.

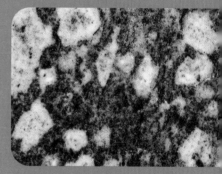

This micrograph shows the minerals in roughly equal proportions.

Diorite can be extremely tough and was used in ancient times to make tools, such as this Neolithic axe head.

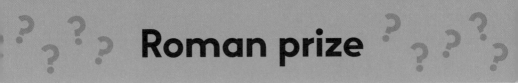

What **rock** is this?

Was this rock used to make **sculptures**?

Why was the purple variety of this rock prized by Roman **emperors**?

What **colors** can it be?

The name of this rock is used to describe rocks formed in **lava**. True or false?

How was the green variety of this rock used in ancient **Rome**?

Porphyry

Porphyries form when crystallization begins deep in Earth's crust and cooling occurs quickly after the rapid upward movement of magma. Historically, the name porphyry was used for the purple-red form of the rock. Many Egyptian, Roman, and Greek sculptures used this type of porphyry.

Type Extrusive

Grain size $\frac{1}{256}$ in (0.1 mm); phenocrysts up to $\frac{3}{4}$ in (2 cm)

Major minerals Various

Minor minerals Various

Color Red, green, purple

Green porphyry was used in ancient Rome in buildings, columns, and statues.

Imperial Porphyry was much prized by Roman emperors as purple was the color of authority.

The clothing of this statue is carved from Imperial Porphyry from Egypt.

Volcanic rock

What **rock** is this?

What **color** is this rock?

Is this rock found on other **planets**?

What is its **grain** size?

Is it a **rare** rock?

What sort of **pattern** can it create on land?

Basalt

Basalt is the most common rock on Earth's surface. It makes up large parts of the ocean floor, and can form volcanic islands when it erupts from volcanoes in ocean basins. The rock has also created huge plateaus on land, and can form hexagonal columns as it cools and cracks, such as the Giant's Causeway in Northern Ireland.

Type Mafic, volcanic

Grain size Less than 1/256 in (0.1 mm)

Major minerals Sodium plagioclase, pyroxene, olivine

Minor minerals Leucite, nepheline, augite

Color Dark gray to black

This basalt calendar is about 11 ft (3.5 m) wide. It was carved by the Aztec people of Mexico.

This temple at Ellora Caves, India, was carved out of solid basalt.

The volcanoes on Mars and Venus are probably made of basalt.

Rare rock

What **rock** is this?

What **colors** can it be?

Where is this rock **found**?

This rock is named after a city in which **country**?

Mining this rock has created the biggest **artificial holes** in the world. True or false?

What important **gemstone** can be mined from it?

Kimberlite

Kimberlite is a rare rock, best known for being the major source of diamonds. Kimberlite is found in dykes and carrot-shaped pipes called diatremes, up to $\frac{5}{8}$ mile (1 kilometer) in diameter. When fresh, it is a blue-green color, but it weathers to yellow.

Type Silica-poor, volcanic

Grain size Wide range

Major minerals Olivine, pyroxene, mica, garnet, diopside

Minor minerals Ilmenite, diamond, serpentine, calcite, rutile, perovskite, magnetite

Color Dark gray

The process of mining kimberlites for their diamonds, as here in Kimberley, South Africa, has resulted in some of the biggest and deepest artificial holes in the world.

Diamonds are rough chunks when mined, only taking on their characteristic sparkle when they are cut and polished into gems.

Kimberlite is named after the town of Kimberley in South Africa, where it was first found.

Gas bubbles

What **rock** is this?

Does it sink or float in **water**?

Is it **smooth** to the touch?

How is it **formed**?

How did the ancient **Romans** use this rock?

What **major** mineral does this rock contain?

Pumice

A porous and froth-like volcanic glass, pumice is created when gas-filled liquid magma erupts like a fizzy drink from a shaken bottle and cools quickly. The resulting foam solidifies into a rock that is full of gas bubbles. Pumice has a low density due to these air-filled pores, which means it can easily float on water.

Type Volcanic

Grain size Less than 1/256 in (0.1 mm)

Major minerals Glass

Minor minerals Feldspar, augite, hornblende, zircon

Color Black, white, yellow, brown

Because pumice is abrasive, it can be used to remove rough skin, especially from your feet!

The ancient Romans used pumice to make concrete, so they could build tall buildings like the Colosseum.

Volcanic glass

What **rock** is this?

What **colors** can it be?

How is it **formed**?

What **minor** minerals does this rock contain?

The people of the Aztec Empire **polished** this rock to make what?

What can cause it to have a **golden** sheen?

Obsidian

The natural volcanic glass obsidian forms when lava solidifies so quickly that crystals do not have time to grow. Obsidian is typically jet black, although the presence of hematite (iron oxide) can result in red and brown varieties. The inclusion of tiny gas bubbles can create a golden sheen.

Type Feldspar-rich, volcanic

Grain size Not granular

Major minerals Glass

Minor minerals Hematite, feldspar

Color Black, red, brown

The people of the Aztec Empire polished this glass-like rock to make mirrors, which they believed were magical.

In snowflake obsidian, clusters of light-colored, needle-like crystals of cristobalite on broken surfaces resemble snowflakes.

This Aztec macuahuitl (war club) is about 30 in (76 cm) long. It has grooved sides set with sharp obsidian blades.

What **rock** is this?

What is its **grain** size?

What **major** mineral does this rock contain?

Where is it **formed**?

This rock is found on **Mars**. True or false?

Is this rock used in **carvings**?

Anorthosite

Anorthosite is coarse-grained and either white or gray, but some rocks can also be green. Anorthosite forms deep in Earth's crust. It is not common at the surface, but when it does appear, it is usually as an enormous mass. It is, however, common on the Moon—the bright areas of the Moon's surface, called the highlands, are made of anorthosite.

Type Ultramafic, plutonic

Grain size $\frac{1}{16}$–$\frac{3}{16}$ in (2–5 mm)

Major minerals Calcium plagioclase

Minor minerals Olivine, pyroxene, garnet

Color Light gray to white, green

Labradorite can be found in anorthosite. Shown here is gemstone labradorite, which is known for its rich play of iridescent colors.

The Apollo 16 astronauts brought back a sample of anorthosite, which is more than 4 billion years old.

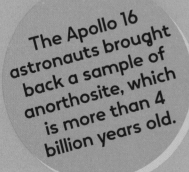

Labradorite is used in carvings as it adds depth.

Extremely tough

What **rock** is this?

What is another **name** for it?

Which ancient **monument** in England was built with this rock?

What **minor** minerals does this rock contain?

How is it used in its **rough** state?

Can you see the **crystals** in this rock with the naked eye?

Dolerite

An extremely hard and tough rock, dolerite is often polished for use as a decorative stone. In its rough state, it is used for paving and is crushed for road stone. Dolerite is also known as black granite. You can see the crystals in dolerite with the naked eye.

Type Mafic, plutonic

Grain size $\frac{1}{256}$–$\frac{1}{16}$ in (0.1–2 mm)

Major minerals Calcium plagioclase, pyroxene

Minor minerals Quartz, magnetite, olivine

Color Dark gray to black, often mottled white

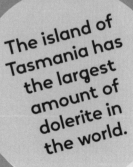

The island of Tasmania has the largest amount of dolerite in the world.

The inner circle at Stonehenge in England is made up of about 80 pieces of dolerite.

Layered rock

What **rock** is this?

Is it characterized by **bands** of minerals?

Is it found on the exterior or core of **mountain** ranges?

The layers of this rock squash into folds or other **patterns** as it forms. True or false?

What **major** minerals does this rock contain?

Does this rock form under high **temperatures**?

Gneiss

Distinct bands of minerals of different colors and grain sizes characterize this metamorphic rock. These bands are mostly folded. Gneiss makes up the cores of many mountain ranges. It forms from sedimentary or granitic rocks at very high pressures and temperatures (1,065°F/573°C or above).

Type Regional metamorphic

Grain size $\frac{1}{16}$–$\frac{3}{16}$ in (2–5 mm)

Major minerals Quartz, feldspar

Minor minerals Biotite, hornblende, garnet, staurolite

Color Gray, pink, multicolored

Gneiss can contain large crystals of metamorphic minerals such as garnet.

This gneiss rock has been eroded and polished by river water rushing past. This reveals the bands of different minerals that have separated and folded into layers.

Wrinkled stone

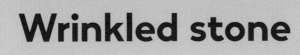

What **rock** is this?

Does it have **layers**?

What is its **grain** size?

What **reflective** mineral is usually present in this rock?

Is it found in **Europe**?

What **colors** can it be?

Schist

Schist is a metamorphic rock with a schistose texture, that is, sheets that are wrinkled, wavy, or irregular. Schist shows distinct layering of light- and dark-colored minerals. The minerals vary, but mica is usually present. The rock color depends on the minerals.

Type Regional metamorphic

Grain size $1/256$ – $1/16$ in (0.1–2 mm)

Major minerals Quartz, feldspar, mica

Minor minerals Garnet, hornblende, actinolite, graphite, kyanite

Color Silvery, green, blue

Tightly folded silver-gray schist can be seen in this outcrop in the European Alps.

This carving in schist shows a bridal procession. It dates to the Kushan Empire (c.30–240 CE).

Schist often contains mica, which is reflective and can make the schist sparkle.

Chalkboard material

What **rock** is this?

Is it usually a light or dark **color**?

It **splits** easily into sheets. True or false?

Does it contain **quartz**?

What is it **used** for?

What can be found **preserved** in this rock?

Slate

Slate is a popular building material, and has many uses. It is known for the way it splits easily into sheets. The color is usually dark—gray, black, green, purple, or red. Slate is a very fine-grained rock, but may contain coarser crystals, such as pyrite. Plant and animal fossils can be preserved in slate.

Type Regional metamorphic

Grain size Less than 1/256 in (0.1 mm)

Major minerals Quartz, mica, feldspar

Minor minerals Pyrite, graphite

Color Various

The minerals in slate are stacked up like the pages of a book.

Originally, pieces of slate were used as chalkboards to write on.

Slate splits easily into thin sheets, which makes it ideal as a durable roofing material.

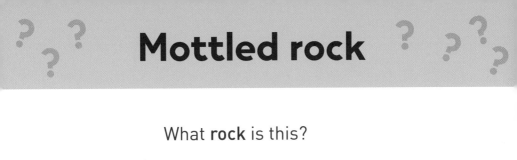

What **rock** is this?

What is it **used** for?

Can it be easily **polished**?

It is often characterized by green and yellow **bands**. True or false?

Where is this rock **formed**?

Serpentinite

This rock forms deep within Earth's crust, where tectonic plates meet. Resembling snakeskin in appearance, serpentinite has flowing bands of various colors, especially green and yellow. It is used as a decorative stone since it can be easily cut and polished.

Type Regional

Grain size Less than $\frac{1}{256}$ in (0.1 mm)

Major minerals Serpentine

Minor minerals Chromite, magnetite, talc

Color Medium to dark

Serpentinite is the state rock of California.

Shown here is an example of a serpentinite rock that is streaked with white veins of calcite.

Greasy feel

What **rock** is this?

Is it a **hard** rock?

What **major** mineral does it contain?

What **colors** can it be?

What is it commonly **used** for?

Are the **grains** fine or coarse?

Soapstone

A massive, fine-grained rock easily recognized by its softness, soapstone has a greasy feel and can be scratched with a fingernail. This is because talc, one of the softest minerals, is its main component.

Type Regional

Grain size Less than $\frac{1}{256}$ in (0.1 mm)

Major minerals Talc

Minor minerals Chlorite, magnesite

Color White, green, brown, black

Since prehistory, soapstone has been used for carvings and utensils.

This ancient vessel was carved from one of the many forms of soapstone used by the craftsmen in Ur (in present-day Iraq) in the 3rd millennium BCE.

Soapstone is a popular material for modern African art, such as this rhinoceros sculpture from Kenya, because it can be carved and cut easily.

Majestic stone

What **rock** is this?

What **colors** can it be?

What famous **monument** is built from this rock?

What well-known **sculpture** is carved from this rock?

Can it be **cut** easily?

Quartz is the dominant mineral in this rock. True or false?

Marble

A granular rock that comes from limestone or dolomite, marble consists of a mass of interlinked calcite or dolomite grains. Marble can be cut relatively easily into slabs, making beautiful stones that are sturdy enough to build with. Pure marble is white.

Type Regional or contact metamorphic

Grain size Up to ¾ in (2 cm)

Major minerals Calcite

Minor minerals Diopside, tremolite, actinolite, dolomite

Color White, pink

Some of the world's most famous sculptures, like Michelangelo's David, are carved from marble.

The Taj Mahal in India is built of makrana—a white marble that changes hue with the angle of the light.

What **major** minerals does it contain?

What **rock** is this?

Does it have **smooth** grains?

Has this rock been found on **Venus**?

What is this rock **made** from?

Can it be **carved**?

Breccia

This rock is made from the broken fragments of other rocks. It can form in several ways. Rocks can shatter—for example, due to frost or earth movement—and the fragments then become cemented in the new position. The grains are sharp and angular rather than smooth and rounded.

Type Detrital, from coarse sediment

Grain size $\frac{1}{16}$ in (2 mm) to 1 in (several cm) in finer matrix

Major minerals Any hard mineral can be present

Minor minerals Any mineral can be present

Color Varies

This ancient Egyptian carved vase made of breccia was used to store liquids.

A basketball-size breccia fragment was found on the Moon by an astronaut in 1971.

It is a **rare** rock.
True or false?

What **rock**
is this?

How is it **used**?

There are 4,000 **arches** made of this
rock in Utah. True or false?

What is its
grain size?

What **color** is it?

Sandstone

The second most abundant sedimentary rock after shale, sandstone makes up 10 to 20 percent of the sedimentary rocks in Earth's crust. Sandstones are classified by their different textures, which form from the way the sand-sized grains are cemented together. Sandstone is used as a building stone because it is durable.

Type Detrital, from sand

Grain size $\frac{1}{256}$–$\frac{1}{16}$ in (0.1–2 mm)

Major minerals Quartz, feldspar

Minor minerals Silica, calcium carbonate

Color Cream to red

A rare type of sandstone found in India can be bent in your hands.

This statue of an Egyptian priest was carved from a single piece of sandstone around 1100 BCE.

This delicate arch is one of 2,000 sandstone rock arches in Utah.

Super abundant

What **rock** is this?

Does it have small **grains**?

It forms on the bottom of **oceans** and **rivers**. True or false?

Is it found in Earth's **crust**?

What is often **preserved** in this rock?

What **fuel** sources can be found in this rock?

Shale

The most abundant sedimentary rock, shale makes up about 70 percent of all sedimentary rocks in Earth's crust. Shales consist of silt- and clay-sized particles deposited by gentle currents on deep ocean floors, shallow sea basins, and river floodplains. They are found between layers of sandstone or limestone.

Type Detrital, from mud, clay, or organic material

Grain size Less than $\frac{1}{256}$ in (0.1 mm)

Major minerals Clays, quartz, calcite

Minor minerals Pyrite, iron oxides, feldspar

Color Various

Preserved in gray shale, this fossil trilobite is more than 400 million years old.

Shale is a source of gas and oil, such as petroleum, which can be made into fuel.

Cracked surface

What **rock** is this?

What does it **look** like?

Can you name one of the **minerals** it contains?

What can be **found** in this rock?

Does it have large or small **grains**?

How **thick** can a deposit of this rock be?

Mudstone

A gray or black rock formed from mud, mudstone contains carbon-rich matter, clay minerals, and detrital minerals such as quartz and feldspar. Mudstones look like hardened clay, and can show the cracks seen in sun-baked clay deposits. Mudstone deposits may be up to several meters thick.

Type Detrital, from mud

Grain size Less than $\frac{1}{256}$ in (0.1 mm)

Major minerals Clays, quartz, calcite

Minor minerals Pyrite, iron oxides, feldspar

Color Various

The grains of mudstone are so fine that they cannot be seen with the naked eye.

Numerous invertebrate fossils can be seen in this mudstone specimen.

This fossil nautilus is preserved in mudstone. The iridescence of its shell is still visible.

Dirty sandstone

What **rock** is this?

What **major** minerals does it contain?

How is it **formed**?

It was used in **ancient Greece** to make coffins and statues. True or false?

It is a mix of **sand** and **mud**. True or false?

Graywacke

Graywacke is a turbidite—a sedimentary rock formed by undersea avalanches. It is a mixture of sand and smaller amounts of mud. Also called dirty sandstone, graywacke is a dark-colored rock. In ancient Egypt, this hard stone was used to make coffins and statues.

Type Detrital, from muddy sand

Grain size $1/256$–$1/16$ in (0.1–2 mm)

Major minerals Quartz, feldspar, mafic minerals

Minor minerals Chlorite, biotite, clay, calcite

Color Mostly gray; also brown, yellow, or black

Graywacke has a typically dirty appearance. Its grains vary in shape and size.

Greywacke gets its name from the German word grauwacke, meaning a gray, earthy rock.

This ancient Egyptian graywacke carving shows Pharaoh Menkaure.

What **rock** is this?

It is always **gray-colored**. True or false?

It has many **uses**—can you name a few?

Where is it usually **formed**?

Can it be **carved**?

Does this rock consist mainly of **calcite**?

Limestone

Limestone is largely made up of calcium carbonate. It generally forms in warm, shallow seas, when marine organisms die and fragments of shell, skeleton, and coral break down into sediment. It is used as a base for roads, a construction material, a white pigment, or a filler in paints, plastics, and toothpaste.

Type Chemical, organic

Grain size Various, from less than $\frac{1}{256}$ in (0.1 mm) to visible particles

Major minerals Calcite

Minor minerals Aragonite, dolomite, siderite, quartz, pyrite

Color White, gray, pink

Fossils in limestone are the remains of ancient sea animals.

Limestone was used in many ancient carvings. Finely detailed statues, such as this one from 2nd-century CE Palmyra (in present-day Syria), were carved out of limestone.

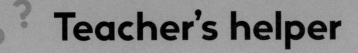

Teacher's helper

What **rock** is this?

What is its **grain** size?

In what **time period** was it formed?

What **color** is this rock?

How is it **used**?

How is it used in **agriculture**?

Chalk

Extensive chalk deposits were formed during the Cretaceous period (145 to 66 million years ago); the name comes from the Latin word *creta*, which means "chalk." Chalk is used to make lime and cement, and as a fertilizer. It is also used as a filler or pigment in a wide variety of materials, including cosmetics.

Type Chemical, organic

Grain size Less than $\frac{1}{256}$ in (0.1 mm)

Major minerals Calcite

Minor minerals Quartz, glauconite, clays

Color White, gray, buff

This specimen of red chalk takes its color from the hematite within it.

Most chalk was formed when dinosaurs were still alive.

Chalk has been compressed into sticks for writing on blackboards since the 19th century.

What **rock** is this?

How is it **formed**?

What **color** is it?

It is sometimes **stained** green by iron oxides. True or false?

What **minor** mineral does it contain?

Tufa

Tufa is formed when lime-rich water evaporates, leaving behind calcium carbonate. It gets deposited on cliffs, caves, and rock surfaces in regions where rainfall is low. In the process of formation, some pebbles and grains of sediment also get caught in it.

Type Chemical

Grain size Less than $\frac{1}{32}$ in (1 mm)

Major minerals Calcite or silica

Minor minerals Aragonite

Color White

This tufa rock formation is in the Rhodope Mountains, Bulgaria. It is locally called the Stone Wedding.

Tufa is often stained red by the presence of iron oxides.

Metal element

What **mineral** is this?

Is it **metallic** looking?

What famous **statue** in the USA is made from the metal?

The metal is the most widely used material for **electrical wiring**. True or false?

When it reacts with air a gray-green **layer** forms. What is it called?

Is it **hard** or **soft**?

Where is it **found**?

Copper

Copper has been used since ancient times. It is found as a native mineral, or is extracted from its many ores. Soft and easily shaped, this metal forms a variety of useful alloys when mixed with other metals. It is an excellent conductor of electricity, and is used to carry electrical current.

Location Chile, USA, Indonesia

Color Orange-red

Luster Metallic

Hardness 2.5–3

Streak Rose

Pure copper reacts with air over time to form a layer of gray-green copper carbonate called verdigris. This can be seen on copper statues, such as the Statue of Liberty in New York City.

Pure copper is mainly used as wires in electrical equipment.

Copper was the first metal to be used by humans.

Silvery shine

What **mineral** is this?

Is it **glassy** or **metallic** looking?

Does it **stay** shiny?

It was first **discovered** in North America. True or false?

What **color** is it?

How is it used in a **fuel** cell?

What does its **name** mean?

Platinum

Spanish explorers first found platinum in the mines of South America in the 1700s. They obtained a whitish substance that the people living near there called *platina*, meaning "little silver". Platinum plays an important role in various technologies.

Location South Africa, Russia, Canada

Color White, silver gray, steel gray

Luster Metallic

Hardness 3.5

Streak Whitish steel gray

This fuel cell contains platinum, which speeds up the reaction between hydrogen and oxygen.

Traces of platinum have been found in Egyptian tombs dated 1200 BCE.

Jewelry made of platinum does not lose its shine.

Brittle metal

What **mineral** is this?

What **color** is it?

The native form of this mineral is common in the **Earth's crust**. True or false?

This mineral can be used to form which **alloy**?

Does it **shatter** easily?

What is the name of this mineral when it is found in **meteorites**?

What did **Vikings** use it for?

Iron

Five percent of Earth's crust is made up of iron. Native iron is rare in the crust, and is nearly always alloyed with nickel. Low-nickel iron (up to 7.5 percent nickel) is called kamacite, and high-nickel iron (up to 50 percent nickel) is called taenite. A third form of iron-nickel, mainly found in meteorites, is called tetrataenite.

Location Worldwide

Color Varied

Luster Metallic

Hardness 4

Streak Steel gray

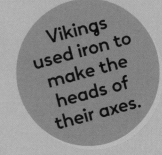

Vikings used iron to make the heads of their axes.

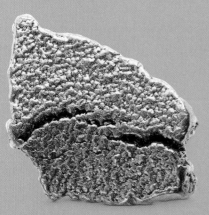

Pure iron is a brittle metal that can shatter easily.

To make iron tougher, tiny amounts of carbon and other metals are added to it. This forms an alloy called steel. These transmission towers are made from steel girders.

Highly prized

What **mineral** is this?

Is this mineral **hard**?

Why is it **highly** sought-after?

It **tarnishes** easily. True or false?

In what form is this mineral mostly **found**?

What **color** is it?

Gold

Gold is the most sought-after mineral in the world, prized for its beauty and rarity. It keeps its soft, yellow sheen because it does not corrode or tarnish easily. Although some lucky people find gold nuggets or crystals, most gold is found as flakes or grains in river silt, where it has washed out of rocks.

Location Worldwide

Color Golden yellow

Luster Metallic

Hardness 2.5–3

Streak Golden yellow

Gold compounds are even used in medicines!

This Egyptian pharaoh's burial mask has kept its soft sheen for more than 3,000 years.

Twisted wires

What **mineral** is this?

Is this a **precious** metal?

What color **streak** does it leave?

What country is the largest **producer** of it?

How is this mineral generally found in its **native** form?

This mineral does not **tarnish**. True or false?

Silver

Silver is a precious metal. Found in our planet's crust as both an ore mineral and in its pure native form, it has been mined since ancient times. However, unlike gold, silver nuggets are very rare. Although most silver is found in ores, native silver forms as crystals, and as twisted wires in rocks.

Location Mexico is the greatest single producer

Color Silver

Luster Metallic

Hardness 2.5–3

Streak Silver white

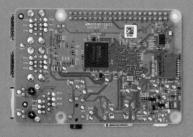

Silver is a natural conductor of electricity, and is used in circuit boards.

Silver is used to make solar power panels.

The bright surface of silver tarnishes after reacting with air.

What **mineral** is this?

Is it a **hard** mineral?

Is it **shiny** or **dull** looking?

Is it formed **underground**?

In what **country** was this mineral first found?

This mineral is always **precious**. True or false?

Diamond

Diamond is the hardest known material in the world. It is lustrous, bright, and resistant to dulling or scratching. Diamonds are formed in Earth's mantle, 87-118 miles (140-190 km) underground. Most diamonds are slightly yellow to brown, due to nitrogen impurities or other defects. Pure diamonds are colorless.

Location Worldwide

Color All colors

Luster Adamantine

Hardness 10

Streak Will scratch streak plate

The famous Koh-I-Noor diamond comes from India, the earliest source of this mineral.

The 45.5-carat Hope Diamond is probably the world's most famous diamond. The blue color is caused by tiny amounts of boron.

Not all diamonds are precious. Bort is an industrial-grade, non-gem diamond that is crushed to make cutting tools and wheels.

Treacherous crystals

What **mineral** is this?

Is it **metallic** looking?

What is the usual **color** of this mineral?

Is it found in **meteorites**?

This mineral can also be ruby **red**. True or false?

Can it be **mistaken** for other minerals?

Sphalerite

Sphalerite takes its name from the Greek *sphaleros*, meaning "treacherous," referring to the fact that it occurs in a number of forms that can be mistaken for other minerals. Its usual color is greenish yellow, but it can also be ruby red.

Location Russia, Spain, Mexico, Canada, USA

Color Yellow green, red, brown, black

Luster Resinous to adamantine, metallic

Hardness 3.5–4

Streak Brownish to light yellow

The stone can easily shatter into small pieces during cutting. For this reason, stones are faceted only for collectors.

Sphalerite is also found in small amounts in meteorites and lunar rock.

This specimen shows the brilliant red crystals of ruby blende sphalerite.

Fool's gold

What **mineral** is this?

Is this mineral **valuable**?

It is only found in **Australia**.
True or false?

Is it **metallic**
looking?

Where does its
name come from?

Can it be used
in **jewelry**?

Pyrite

Pyrite is a bright and shiny pretender. If you are not careful, it will trick you into thinking that you have struck gold. However, pyrite will not make you rich. It contains nothing of value, except perhaps some iron. Pyrite gets its name from the Greek word *pyr*, meaning "fire," because pyrite gives off sparks when struck by iron.

Location Worldwide

Color Pale brass yellow

Luster Metallic

Hardness 6–6.5

Streak Greenish black to brownish black

With care, brittle pyrite can be ground into beads, such as those strung together in this necklace.

The gleaming gold crystals are known as "fool's gold" because of their power to dazzle.

Pyrite has replaced this shell's minerals during fossilization.

What **mineral** is this?

In which **countries** is this mineral found?

Does it look **shiny** or **dull**?

What **year** was it discovered?

How is it **used**?

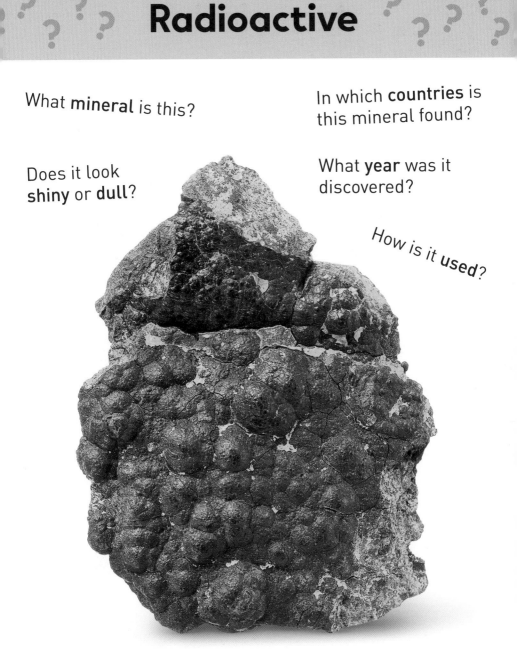

You have to be **careful** when handling this mineral. True or false?

Which famous **physicists** worked with this mineral?

Uraninite

Discovered by the German chemist M. H. Klaproth in 1789, uraninite is a major ore of uranium. It is black to brownish black, dark gray, or greenish. Uraninite is used in the making of nuclear bombs, and as fuel for nuclear reactors, which generate electricity.

Location Finest found in Czech Republic, Germany, The Democratic Republic of the Congo, USA, Canada

Color Black, brownish black, dark gray, greenish

Luster Submetallic, pitchy, dull

Hardness 5–6

Streak Brownish black

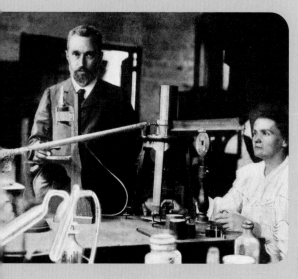

The pioneering work on radioactivity by physicists Pierre and Marie Curie was based on uranium extracted from uraninite ores.

The ore from this rock is highly radioactive and must be handled professionally with care!

Ruby copper

What **mineral** is this?

It can be **transparent**.
True or false?

Where in the **world**
is it found?

Is it an **ore**
of iron?

Does it have a
green **streak**?

How does the
color of this rock
change?

Cuprite

A soft, heavy, copper oxide, cuprite is an important ore of copper. Its crystals are often striated. Cuprite is translucent and bright red when freshly broken, but turns to a dull metallic gray color when it is exposed to light and pollutants.

Location Namibia, Australia, Bolivia, Chile

Color Shades of red to nearly black

Luster Adamantine, submetallic

Hardness 3.5–4

Streak Brownish red, shining

Rare transparent cuprite is sometimes cut for collectors.

Cuprite is sometimes known as ruby copper due to its distinctive red color.

This cuprite specimen has a large number of minute crystals, and exhibits a rare form of fibrous cuprite, chalcotrichite.

What **mineral** is this?

It has a brown **streak**.
True or false?

Does it **rust**?

Does it have a
metallic appearance?

What **metal** is
it a source of?

It is used to **make**
many things—can
you name one?

Chromite

Chromite is the world's most important source of chromium. It is used to make gleaming, chrome-plated bathroom taps, car parts, and kitchen appliances, and is also added to steel to make it super hard. Chromite occurs in sedimentary layers or in weathered nodules within a rock.

Location Most common in South Africa

Color Dark brown, black

Luster Metallic

Hardness 5.5

Streak Brown

The metal stays shiny even when exposed to air and water.

Chromium is an important pigment in many types of paint, ink, dye, and cosmetics.

The chromium plating protects this motorcycle from rusting.

Glowing light

What **mineral** is this?

Does this mineral have a **glassy** or **metallic** appearance?

Is it found in a wide **range** of colors?

Why is it found in **toothpaste**?

What did the **ancient Egyptians** make with it?

Is it often used in **jewelry**?

What happens to it under **ultraviolet** light?

Fluorite

Fluorite has one of the widest color ranges of any mineral, with violet, green, and yellow being the most common. Zones of different colors occur within a single crystal. The ancient Egyptians carved massive fluorite into statues and scarabs, and the Chinese used it in carvings for more than 300 years.

Location Worldwide

Color Colorless, blue, green, purple, orange, yellow

Luster Glassy

Hardness 4

Streak White

Toothpaste contains fluoride, which strengthens tooth enamel.

When seen under ultraviolet light, fluorite is fluorescent (it gives off a glowing light).

This necklace is composed of beads of green and purple fluorite. Although fluorite is rarely used in jewelry as it fractures easily, it can be worn as beads.

Cubic crystals

What **mineral** is this?

What other **name** is it known by?

How is it used on **roads**?

It has been used as a **currency** in the past. True or false?

Does it **dissolve** in water?

Is this mineral **formed** above ground or below ground?

Halite

Salt is a halide mineral made of sodium chloride, which has been mined and traded since ancient times. Rock salt, also known as halite, forms in vast deposits underground. Since most halides dissolve in water (they make sea water salty), deposits of these minerals occur in dry places where water evaporates.

Location Russia, France, India, Canada, USA

Color Usually colorless or white

Luster Glassy

Hardness 2.5

Streak White

Mined since ancient times and also used as a currency, common table salt is the mineral halite.

Halite is used to make soap and glass.

Spraying salt keeps roads free from ice and frost.

Digestive salt

What **mineral** is this?

What **streak** does it have?

How is it used by **gardeners**?

What other **name** is it called?

Where was it first **discovered**?

It can be found in **caves**. True or false?

Sylvite

The name sylvite comes from its Latin medicinal name, *sal digestivus sylvii*, which means "digestive salt." Sylvite is also known as sylvine. It is found in thick beds mixed with halite and other evaporite minerals. It also forms in volcanic fumaroles and caves.

Location USA, Canada, Germany

Color Usually colorless or white

Luster Glassy

Hardness 2.5

Streak White

Sylvite is used as a fertilizer to help plants grow.

The mineral was first discovered in 1823 on Mount Vesuvius, Italy, where it was found on lava.

What **mineral** is this?

Does this mineral have a **metallic** appearance?

It is used to make **medicines**. True or false?

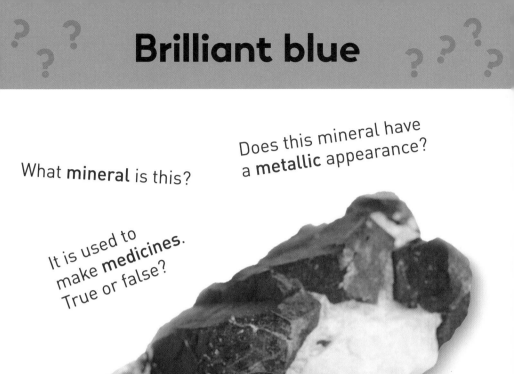

Where in the **world** are the best crystals of this mineral found?

Which **pigment** is this mineral used to make?

In which rock is this the **main** mineral?

Lazurite

This rare mineral forms in limestone and it is the main mineral in lapis lazuli—a rock prized for its use in carvings, medicines, cosmetics, and jewelry for thousands of years. Lazurite is also the main ingredient of a brilliant blue pigment called ultramarine. The best lazurite crystals come from Afghanistan.

Location Finest found in Afghanistan

Color Blue

Luster Dull to glassy

Hardness 5–5.5

Streak Bright blue

Lazurite's name comes from the Arabic word lazaward, which means "heaven" or "sky."

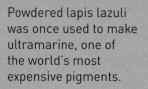

Powdered lapis lazuli was once used to make ultramarine, one of the world's most expensive pigments.

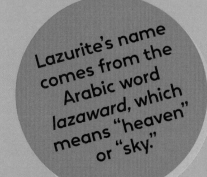

This carving made of Afghan lapis lazuli shows an adult and two baby tortoises.

Bad smell

What **mineral** is this?

Is it difficult to **break**?

It has a black **streak**.
True or false?

Does it glow under
ultraviolet light?

What **color** is this
mineral?

What food can it
smell like if you
break it?

Sodalite

Sodalite is a deep-blue colored mineral that contains the metal sodium. Like halite (rock salt), which is also made of sodium, sodalite is light, and breaks easily, so it often contains many cracks. It is one of the minerals found inside the rock lapis lazuli.

Location Russia, Germany, India, Canada, USA

Color Gray, white, blue

Luster Glassy to greasy

Hardness 5.5–6

Streak White to light blue

When illuminated under ultraviolet light, many sodalite pieces fluoresce.

Sodalite often contains sulfur, which can make it smell like rotten eggs if you break it!

Even though sodalite breaks easily, it can be shaped by a skilled carver.

What **mineral** is this?

It is an important source of **gold**. True or false?

Is it difficult to **extract**?

How does it **change** color when exposed to the atmosphere?

Is this mineral found throughout the **world**?

Is it **glassy** or **metallic** looking?

Chalcopyrite

Chalcopyrite is an important ore of copper. It is opaque and brassy yellow when freshly mined, but it commonly develops a shimmering iridescent tarnish when exposed to the atmosphere. It occurs in vast deposits and the copper can be easily extracted.

Location Worldwide

Color Brassy yellow

Luster Metallic

Hardness 3.5–4

Streak Green-black

Chalcopyrite can be mistaken for gold, but it is more brittle.

This freshly mined specimen has an uneven fracture and tetrahedral shape.

An iridescent tarnish covers chalcopyrite when it is exposed to the atmosphere.

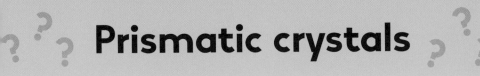

What **mineral** is this?

What **metal** is derived from this mineral?

What color is it when **enclosed** in quartz?

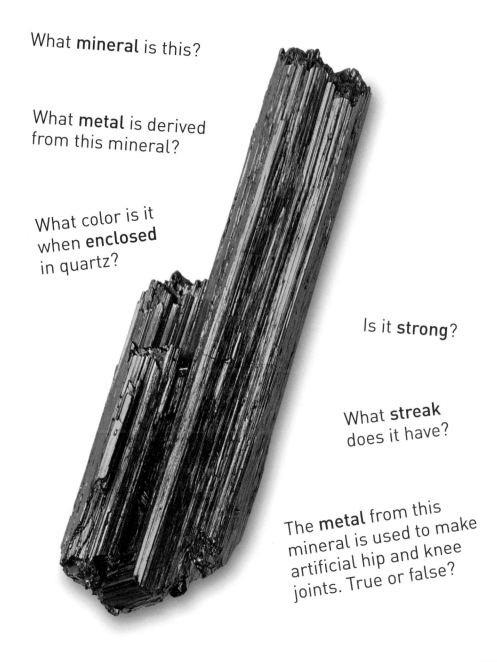

Is it **strong**?

What **streak** does it have?

The **metal** from this mineral is used to make artificial hip and knee joints. True or false?

Rutile

Rutile often appears as pale golden, needle-like crystals inside quartz. When not enclosed in quartz, it is usually yellowish or reddish brown, dark brown, or black. Rutile is a vital part of modern life. Titanium is derived from rutile and is used to make artificial hip and knee joints. It is also used in aircraft construction due to its high strength.

Location Worldwide

Color Red, golden, brown, black

Luster Adamantine to submetallic

Hardness 6–6.5

Streak Pale brown to yellowish

Rutile takes its name from the Latin *rutilis*, which means "red" or "glowing."

Pale golden rutile crystals in polished quartz

Dark-hued crystals in rock groundmass

Flickering color

What **mineral** is this?

This mineral has
a red **streak**.
True or false?

What **metal** is
extracted from
this mineral?

Where does its
name come from?

Where is it
mostly **mined**?

How is it used to
store **food**?

Cassiterite

The tin oxide cassiterite takes its name from the Greek word for tin, *kassiteros*. Also called tinstone, it is colorless when pure, but usually appears brown or black due to iron impurities. Cassiterite is rarely gray or white. It continues to be mined for tin, especially in Malaysia, Thailand, Indonesia, and Bolivia.

Location Worldwide

Color Usually brown or black

Luster Adamantine to metallic

Hardness 6–7

Streak White, grayish, brownish

Cassiterite is important for food storage; it provides us with the tin to make tin cans.

This shows the yellow-brown color typical of most faceted cassiterites. Its color flickers in the light like a diamond.

This specimen displays the yellow variety of tin oxide.

Gold indicator

What **mineral** is this?

Does it have a metallic or greasy **appearance**?

What happens when it is put under **ultraviolet** light?

Where would you find this mineral on a **rocket**?

It can be **transparent**. True or false?

Which **metal** is extracted from this mineral?

Scheelite

Irregular masses of colorless, gray, orange, or pale brown scheelite can be difficult to spot, but they fluoresce vivid bluish white under a shortwave ultraviolet light. Scheelite is sometimes associated with native gold, and its fluorescence is used by geologists in their search for gold deposits.

Location Worldwide

Color Yellow, white, pale green, orange

Luster Glassy to greasy

Hardness 4.5–5

Streak White

Shown below is a transparent scheelite, which is relatively rare. Soft and easily scratched, scheelite is not used for jewelry.

Tungsten from scheelite is used to make rocket nozzles.

Tungsten is refined from scheelite. Tungsten has the highest melting point of any metal and is used in heaters and light bulbs.

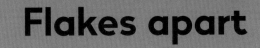

Flakes apart

What **mineral** is this?

Does it have a **glassy** appearance?

What happens to it when **heated**?

This mineral has a black **streak**. True or false?

Which **Greek** words does it take its name from?

Which **country** produces a lot of this mineral?

Tetragonal
Silicates

Apophyllite

The name apophyllite comes from the Greek words *apo* and *phyllazein*, which mean "to get" and "leaf"—a reference to the way in which the mineral separates into flakes or layers when it is heated. Apophyllite specimens are green, pink, colorless, or white. Crystals are transparent or translucent.

Location Worldwide

Color Green, pink, colorless, white

Luster Glassy

Hardness 4.5–5

Streak Colorless

Blocky green crystals

India is a big producer of Apophyllite. Vendors sell it on street corners.

Reddish pink crystals

Sparkling substitute

What **mineral** is this?

Is it **oily** looking?

Is this mineral found in many **colors**?

Is it used in **jewelry**?

What process is used to create a **blue** color?

What other **gem** can it look like?

Zircon

Known since ancient times, zircon takes its name from the Persian words *zar*, which means "gold," and gun, which means "color." Gems can also be colorless, yellow, gray, green, brown, blue, or red. Brown zircon is often heat-treated to turn it blue.

Location Australia, Myanmar, Cambodia, Tanzania

Color Various

Luster Adamantine to oily

Hardness 7.5

Streak White

Zircon often matches diamond in its sparkling brilliance.

This zircon has been heat-treated to intensify its color.

Colorless zircon is often used in jewelry as a substitute for diamonds.

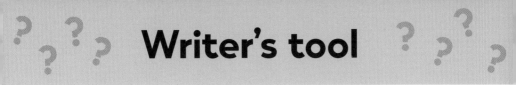

What **mineral** is this?

Is it **hard** or **soft**?

Is it **greasy**?

How is it **used**?

What **element** is it made from?

It can carry **electricity**. True or false?

What **color** is this mineral?

Graphite

The element carbon is found in two forms: diamond, which is the hardest known mineral in the world, and graphite, which is a soft, greasy mineral that has many different uses. Graphite is opaque and dark gray to black. It occurs as hexagonal crystals, flexible sheets, scales, or large masses.

Location Worldwide

Color Dark gray to black

Luster Metallic or dull earthy

Hardness 1–2

Streak Black to steel gray, shiny

The name graphite comes from the Greek word *graphein*, which means "to write".

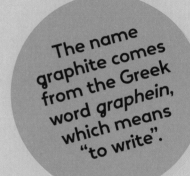

Pencil "lead" contains graphite. The first use of graphite pencils was described in 1575.

This battery has a graphite core that carries electric current.

What **mineral** is this?

It is a **hard** mineral. True or false?

Who is this mineral **named** after?

Is it **iridescent**?

What **metal** is extracted from this mineral?

On which **volcano** was it first discovered?

Covellite

Named in 1832 after the Italian mineralogist Niccolo Covelli, who first described it, covellite is a copper sulfide. A minor ore of copper, covellite is opaque, with a bright metallic blue or indigo color. It is easy to recognize because of its brassy yellow, deep red, or purple iridescence.

Location Worldwide

Color Metallic blue, indigo

Luster Submetallic to resinous

Hardness 1.5–2

Streak Lead gray to black, shiny

Covellite was first found on Mount Vesuvius volcano in Italy.

This specimen shows rare covellite crystals in their tabular habit.

What **mineral** is this?

Does this mineral have a **glassy** appearance?

Is this mineral **poisonous**?

What **metal** is extracted from this mineral?

The powdered form of this mineral was used for the pigment **vermilion**. True or false?

What **color** is this mineral?

Cinnabar

Highly poisonous, cinnabar is the main ore of mercury. It is the central ingredient in the pigment vermilion, and its brilliant orange-red color was used in paintings in ancient China. Cinnabar often forms around volcanic vents and hot springs.

Location Mainly from Spain

Color Orange-red

Luster Adamantine to dull

Hardness 2–2.5

Streak Scarlet

Cinnabar takes its name from the Persian zinjirfrah and Arabic zinjafr, which mean "dragon's blood."

This specimen of massive cinnabar has a nonmetallic, adamantine luster.

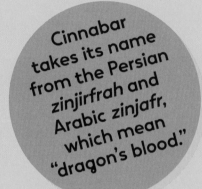

Vermilion was originally made from ground cinnabar.

Golden crystals

What **mineral** is this?

It only forms **single** crystals. True or false?

What color **streak** does it have?

Which **coin** is made from this mineral?

Does this mineral have a **metallic** appearance?

Is this mineral found in **meteorites**?

Where in the **world** is this mineral found?

Millerite

Millerite has delicate, needle-like, opaque golden crystals. It can form freestanding, single crystals, or occur as tufts, matted groups, or radiating sprays. It is massive, and frequently found with an iridescent tarnish. Millerite is also found in meteorites.

Location USA, Canada, Czech Republic, Germany, Slovakia, UK

Color Pale brassy yellow

Luster Metallic

Hardness 3–3.5

Streak Greenish black

Millerite is an ore of nickel, used to make the American coin of the same name.

Thin, radiating crystals of millerite have formed in a hollow space in this geode.

What **mineral** is this?

Is this mineral **hard** or **soft**?

What metal is it a **source** of?

It has a red **streak**. True or false?

When was it **recognized** as a mineral?

How is it used in **engines**?

Molybdenite

Molybdenite is the most important source of molybdenum, which is used to make high-strength steels. Molybdenite was originally thought to be lead, and so its name came from the Greek word for lead, *molybdos*. It was recognized as a distinct mineral by the Swedish chemist Carl Scheele in 1778.

Location USA, China, Chile, Peru

Color Lead gray

Luster Metallic

Hardness 1–1.5

Streak Greenish or bluish gray

Molybdenum has an extremely high melting point of 4,730°F (2,610°C)!

Pure molybdenum is mainly used to make alloys that are resistant to corrosion. These alloys are lightweight, so they are ideal for constructing bicycle frames.

This slippery lubricant, which contains finely powdered molybdenite mixed with oil, protects fast-moving mechanical parts in engines.

Dark ruby silver

What **mineral** is this?

What **metal** is mined from this mineral?

In which **countries** can it be found?

Why does it need to be stored in the **dark**?

Can it be used to make **jewelry**?

Does this mineral have a **metallic** luster?

Pyrargyrite

Also known as dark ruby silver, pyrargyrite takes its name from the Greek words *pyros*, which means "fire," and *argent*, which means "silver"—an allusion to its silver content and its translucent, dark red color. It turns opaque dull gray when exposed to light. Therefore, prized specimens are stored in the dark.

Location Germany, Bolivia, Mexico, USA

Color Deep red

Luster Adamantine

Hardness 2.5

Streak Purplish red

Silver can be found pure in nature, but mostly it is mined from ores such as pyrargyrite.

Pure silver can be molded and cut into varying shapes.

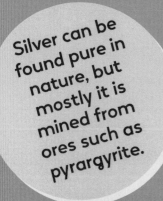

This Roman denarius (silver coin) shows the head of Julius Caesar, the first living Roman to appear on a coin.

Light red silver ore

What **mineral** is this?

Is it **hard** or **soft**?

Which **scientist** is it named after?

Is it **glassy** looking?

Is it a **common** mineral?

The finest minerals are only found in **Chile** and **Germany**. True or false?

Is it popular with **gem collectors**?

Proustite

As its original name ruby silver suggests, proustite is translucent and red, and is an important source of silver. It has also been called light red silver ore. The name proustite comes from the French chemist Joseph Proust, who distinguished it from the related mineral pyrargyrite in 1832.

Location Finest found in Chile and Germany

Color Scarlet, gray

Luster Adamantine to submetallic

Hardness 2–2.5

Streak Vermilion

As a rare and beautiful mineral, proustite is highly sought after by gem collectors.

Its bright ruby-red crystals make attractive gems. Chile and Germany are notable sources of proustite.

Melting mineral

What **mineral** is this?

Does this mineral have a black **streak**?

Is it **glassy** or **metallic** looking?

As a solid, does it form **snowflakes**?

This mineral is usually found in a **liquid** form. True or false?

Is it a **rare** mineral?

Hexagonal
Oxides

Ice

Ice is one of the most abundant minerals on Earth's surface. Like iron ore, ruby, and cuprite, ice is also an oxide. Unlike the other oxides, however, it exists mostly in its liquid form, as water. As a solid, it is found as ice crystals (which form snowflakes, glaciers, and ice caps), icicles, hailstones, and frost.

Location Worldwide

Color Colorless, white

Luster Glassy

Hardness Varies

Streak White

Ice only appears to be white because the gas trapped within it reflects light.

Snowflakes have a symmetrical, six-pointed pattern.

The Arctic Ocean is covered in a 9–13 ft (3–4 m) thick sheet of ice, but much of this melts in summer, cracking up into giant icebergs.

What **mineral** is this?

It is the **hardest** mineral on Earth. True or false?

Does it have a **glassy** appearance?

Is it found throughout the **world**?

What are the **gem** varieties of this mineral called?

Where does its **name** come from?

Corundum

After diamond, corundum is the hardest mineral on Earth. The name corundum comes from the Sanskrit *kuruvinda*, meaning "ruby"—the name given to red corundum. Ruby and sapphire are gem varieties. Corundum is often white, gray, or brown, but gem colors include red ruby, blue, and pink sapphire.

Location Finest found in India, Myanmar, Russia, Zimbabwe, South Africa

Color Various

Luster Adamantine to glassy

Hardness 9

Streak Colorless

At 23.10 carats, this is the largest faceted ruby in the United States National Gem Collection. The stone was mined from the Mogok region of Myanmar in the 1930s.

Impurities in corundum give the stones their colors. Colorless corundum is rare.

Displaying the gem in its natural state, this specimen of rock groundmass is host to a number of ruby crystals.

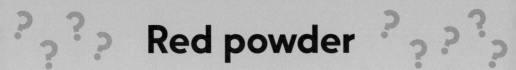

Red powder

What **mineral** is this?

Is it used in **painting**?

Does it have a **glassy** appearance?

What **streak** does it have?

Is it found in **Space**?

This is a **rare** mineral. True or false?

What **metal** is it an ore of?

Hematite

Hematite is derived from the Greek *haimatitis*, meaning "blood-red"—a reference to the red color of its powder. It is an abundant mineral, and an important source of iron ore. The reddish appearance of Mars is due to the presence of hematite on its surface, and is the reason for its nickname, the red planet. In powdered form, Hematite provides the basis for many paints.

Location Worldwide

Color Black, gray, silver, red, brown

Luster Metallic to dull

Hardness 5–6

Streak Red to reddish brown

Pigment made from hematite has been found in cave paintings dating back 40,000 years.

Hematite is a popular, inexpensive carving material for objects such as this frog.

The Wave, in Arizona, USA, is a natural formation of sandstone rocks. The rocks' varied colors are caused by the presence of different minerals, including hematite.

What **mineral** is this?

Does it have a **glassy** appearance?

Can you name one of the five **countries** it is found in?

Is it a **common** mineral?

What creatures have **shells** made from this mineral?

What object made from this mineral was found in Tutankhamun's **tomb**?

Calcite

One of the three most common carbonates on Earth, this calcium carbonate grows anywhere that water can reach. Shellfish make their shells from calcite, which they take from sea water. Calcite is known for its beautiful crystals, and although it can be almost any color, in its pure form it is white or colorless.

Location Iceland, USA, Germany, Czech Republic, Mexico

Color Various

Luster Glassy

Hardness 3

Streak White

Calcite has the largest number of different crystal structures of any mineral.

Ancient Egyptians used calcite for items such as this jar stopper from Tutankhamun's tomb.

Prized blue-green gem

What **mineral** is this?

Does it **chip** easily?

Deposits of this mineral often look like a bunch of which **fruit**?

Who is this mineral **named** after?

What is the most **prized** color?

The anti-itch lotion **calamine** contains this mineral. True or false?

Smithsonite

Smithsonite was originally known as calamine—as in the anti-itch lotion used to treat skin problems, which contains the powdered mineral. The British chemist and mineralogist James Smithson discovered that calamine was in fact three different minerals, and smithsonite was named in his honor in 1832.

Location Worldwide

Color Various

Luster Glassy to pearly

Hardness 4–4.5

Streak White

Smithsonite deposits often look like a bunch of icicles or grapes.

Smithsonite is brittle, soft, and easily chipped, as can be seen at the base of this example. The stone has been polished to reveal its glassy luster.

Smithsonite can be various colors, including yellow and pink, but blue-green is the most prized of all.

Rose-red crystals

What **mineral** is this?

Is this mineral found in **Japan**?

It is sometimes a **blue** color. True or false?

Is it **hard** or **soft**?

What did the people of the **Inca civilization** believe about this mineral?

What **metal** is it an ore of?

Rhodochrosite

This prized collectors' mineral has a rose-pink color, but some rhodochrosite can also be brown or gray. It is a soft and fragile mineral, and is sometimes mined as an ore of manganese. People of the Inca civilization believed that rhodochrosite was the blood of ancient kings and queens that had turned to stone.

Location USA, South Africa, Romania, Gabon, Mexico, Russia, Japan

Color Rose-pink, cherry red

Luster Glassy to pearly

Hardness 3.5–4

Streak White

These two decorative ducks were carved using rhodochrosite for the bodies and calcite for the heads.

Rhodochrosite derives its name from the Greek word rhodokhros, meaning "of rosy color."

The red-pink transparent crystals of rhodochrosite are a good source of manganese, and when alloyed with other metals, manganese can be used to make railway tracks.

What **mineral** is this?

Does it have a **glassy** luster?

What **metal** is it often mixed with?

It was used by ancient metalworkers to make **Damascus steel**. True or false?

What **tools** are made using this mineral?

The finest minerals are found in which two **countries**?

Vanadinite

Vanadium, the ore of vanadinite, was first purified in 1869 by the British chemist Henry Roscoe. Ancient metalworkers used tiny amounts of vanadium compounds to make a very tough substance called Damascus steel. Vanadium is also used in catalysts—compounds that speed up chemical reactions.

Location Finest found in Morocco and USA

Color Orange red, yellow

Luster Adamantine

Hardness 3

Streak Whitish yellow

This Damascus steel knife has been strengthened by the addition of vanadium.

About 85 percent of all vanadium is used to toughen steel.

Tools, such as these wrenches, made with alloys of vanadium and steel are durable.

What **mineral** is this?

This mineral is only found in **one** country. True or false?

Is it found in **sandstone**?

Is it **glassy** or **metallic** looking?

How does the **smoky** version of this mineral get its color?

The purple variety of this mineral is named after which character in **Greek mythology**?

Hexagonal or Trigonal
Silicates

Quartz

Quartz is one of the most common minerals on the surface of Earth. Sand is made up mostly of quartz crystals, and the mineral is found in common rocks, such as granite and sandstone. There are many color varieties of quartz.

Location Worldwide

Color Various

Luster Glassy

Hardness 7

Streak White

Smoky quartz is light brown to black. It gets its color from radioactive damage.

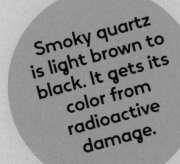

Rose quartz gets its rose-red color from manganese and other metals. Pure crystals of rose quartz are rare.

Amethyst is purple quartz and gets its color from iron impurities. It is named after the maiden Amethyst from Greek mythology.

What **mineral** is this?

What are the main **gemstone** varieties of this mineral?

Is this mineral **hard** or **soft**?

This mineral is the source of which **metal**?

It has a green **streak**. True or false?

Can this mineral be found in **granite**?

Beryl

Few people have heard of the mineral beryl, but almost everyone has heard of its principal gemstone varieties—emerald and aquamarine. The mineral is also the source of one of the modern world's most important metals—beryllium.

Location Worldwide

Color Colorless, red, blue, green, yellow

Luster Glassy

Hardness 7.5–8

Streak White

Most beryl is found in granites, granite pegmatites, and rhyolites, but it can also occur in metamorphic rocks, such as schists.

Emeralds have been highly prized since they were first mined in Egypt in 1300 BCE.

Emeralds are one of the most desirable gemstones.

Red-spotted

What **mineral** is this?

What **color** is this mineral?

Does it have a **glassy** appearance?

What other **name** is it known by?

It gets its **name** from the blood-red flecks of jasper. True or false?

Is it found in **Australia**?

Bloodstone

Also called heliotrope, bloodstone is colored by traces of iron silicates, and has patches of bright red jasper—it gets its name from these blood-red flecks. Bloodstone is deposited as silica-rich waters at low temperatures (up to 400°F/200°C) filter through cracks and fissures.

Location Mostly India, Brazil, Australia, USA

Color Green with red spots

Luster Glassy

Hardness 6.5–7

Streak Colorless

Bloodstone was one of the first gems to be used by humans.

The ancient Romans carved bloodstone into cameos. These are raised designs, often of people, cut into gems.

Striped gemstone

What **mineral** is this?

Does it have a **metallic** appearance?

What is the variety with white and red **bands** known as?

The **black** variety of this mineral is the most common. True or false?

Where does its **name** come from?

What **streak** does it have?

Onyx

Onyx is a semiprecious variety of agate with straight bands of black and white. Its varieties include carnelian onyx, which has white and red bands, and sardonyx, with white and reddish-brown bands. Its layers of contrasting colors make it popular for use in jewelry.

Location Mainly India and South America

Color White color-banded

Luster Glassy

Hardness 7

Streak White

This gold pendant has an unusual solid black onyx gemstone— natural black onyx is very rare.

The name onyx comes from the Greek word onux, which means "nail" or "claw."

This cameo brooch of a classical figure has been carved out of sardonyx.

Bands of color

What **mineral** is this?

It is always a **red** color.
True or false?

How is this mineral **formed**?

What did people believe it could **cure**?

Is it **glassy** or **metallic** looking?

It can have a moss-like **pattern**.
True or false?

Agate

Agate forms when circulating, mineral-rich fluids deposit silica in cavities in the rock. Quartz is deposited around the inside surface, and builds up in layers that follow the shape of the cavity. As a result, it is characterized by various bands of color, each containing small amounts of different materials such as manganese, iron, or copper.

Location Worldwide

Color Various

Luster Glassy

Hardness 7

Streak White

In the Middle Ages, wearing agate was thought to cure insomnia and ensure sweet dreams.

Impurities give agate lovely colors, such as fire agate, which gets its reddish-brown color from hematite.

The mosslike pattern in this agate is in fact staining from one of the iron or manganese oxides that penetrated the agate after it was formed.

Precious stone

What **mineral** is this?

It was once considered a **lucky stone**. True or false?

Where are most of these **precious stones** found?

How does it **form**?

Does it **reflect** light?

What other **planet** has it been found on?

Amorphous
Silicates

Opal

Opal derives its name from the Latin word *opalus*, which means "precious stone." It sometimes forms when rain drips into rock. The water then carries dissolved minerals into the cracks and, over thousands of years, these grow into an opal. Some of the liquid also remains locked inside the gem.

Location Mostly Ethiopia and Australia

Color Colorless, white, yellow, orange, rose-red, black, dark blue

Luster Glassy

Hardness 5–6

Streak White

Seen from different directions, light is reflected as yellows, oranges, blues, or greens.

Opal that is transparent or translucent red or orange is called "fire" opal.

Photographs of the surface of Mars show there are opals on the red planet.

What **mineral** is this?

This mineral forms a **green** crust when exposed to light. True or false?

What **color** is it?

Where might you find it in a **car**?

It was once used in **fireworks**. True or false?

Is this mineral **poisonous**?

Realgar

This mineral is sometimes called ruby sulfur, or ruby of arsenic. It is an important ore of the poison arsenic—every form of arsenic, either pure or in a compound, is poisonous to animals. When exposed to light, the crystals crumble, and form a yellow crust.

Location Germany, Mexico, Corsica, Romania, USA

Color Scarlet to orange yellow

Luster Resinous to greasy

Hardness 1.5–2

Streak Scarlet to orange yellow

Arsenic is mixed with lead to create a tough alloy that is often used in car batteries.

In the past the Chinese used realgar for carvings, but they deteriorated in the light.

Scarlet to orange-yellow in color, powdered realgar was once used as a pigment and in fireworks.

What **mineral** is this?

Does it have a **greasy** appearance?

Does it have a white **streak**?

What **industry** is it important for?

Where was the largest **deposit** of this mineral found?

It is used in the **production** of which metal?

Cryolite

Few people have heard of cryolite, but it is one of the most important minerals of our age, especially in the engineering industry—aircraft could not fly without it. Cryolite is usually colorless or white. The largest deposit, at Ivigtut in Greenland, is now exhausted. Lesser amounts are found in Spain, Russia, and the USA.

Location Greenland, Spain, Russia, USA

Color Colorless or white

Luster Glassy to greasy

Hardness 2.5

Streak White

Cryolite takes its name from the Greek words kryos and lithos which mean "ice stone."

Synthetic cryolite is an essential ingredient in aluminum production. It is used to separate aluminum—an indispensable metal in aviation—from its ores.

What **mineral** is this?

Is this mineral **hard** or **soft**?

What **Persian** word does it take its name from?

Which **metal** is found inside this mineral?

Over time, the powdered form changes **color**. True or false?

How was this mineral used in **art**?

Azurite

Azurite was used as a blue pigment in 15th- to 17th-century Renaissance European art, and probably in the production of blue glaze in ancient Egypt. It is also one of the sources of copper. Azurite takes its name from the Persian word *lazhuward*, which means "blue."

Location Worldwide

Color Azure to dark blue

Luster Glassy to dull earthy

Hardness 3.5–4

Streak Blue

Due to moisture in the air, powdered azurite used in paintings can turn from blue to green over time.

Azurite and malachite are often mixed, and can make spectacular gems, such as this heart-shaped stone.

When cut in the proper direction, the patterns produced by the vivid blue malachite and green azurite can be stunning.

Green gemstone

Is it easy to **carve**?

What **mineral** is this?

A famous football **trophy** is decorated with this mineral. True or false?

What is one way this mineral was used in ancient **Egypt**?

Is this mineral found in **Australia**?

This mineral shows what **metal** is present?

Malachite

The name malachite comes from a Greek word meaning green, and it is easy to see why. A green crust of malachite is a sign that other copper minerals are present below the surface, and prospectors look for this sign as they survey an area for valuable minerals. Malachite has been used for centuries for making ornaments, and today it is an important gemstone.

Location DR Congo, Australia, Morocco, USA, France

Color Bright green

Luster Adamantine to silky

Hardness 3.5–4

Streak Pale green

The FIFA World Cup trophy is decorated with malachite.

Malachite is quite soft and is easily carved into statues and other ornaments.

Malachite powder was used in ancient Egypt as eyeshadow, pigment for wall painting, and in glazes and colored glass.

Shatterproof

What **mineral** is this?

What **streak** does this mineral have?

Is it **glassy** or **metallic** looking?

Who is it **named** after?

Where in the **world** is it found?

This mineral is an important source of **boron**. True or false?

Colemanite

An important source of boron, colemanite was named in 1884 after William Coleman, the owner of the mine in California, where it was discovered. Borosilicates, which come from colemanite and other minerals, are used to make glass that is resistant to chemicals, electricity, and heat.

Location USA, Chile, and Turkey

Color Colorless, white, yellowish white, gray

Luster Glassy to adamantine

Hardness 4–4.5

Streak White

Borosilicate glass is used in car headlights, laboratory glassware, industrial equipment, and ovenware.

Borosilicate glass can be heated to around 932°F (500°C) without shattering!

Heaps mark the borate mines at Death Valley, California.

What **mineral** is this?

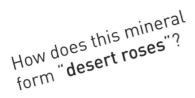
How does this mineral form "**desert roses**"?

What is this mineral called when it is **fine grained**?

Is this a **soft** or **hard** mineral?

What is it used for in our **homes**?

Which **form** of this mineral looks like a ram's horn?

Gypsum

Gypsum is one of the world's most useful minerals. It is used mostly to make the plasterboard that covers the inside walls of our homes. Gypsum crystals form when water containing dissolved calcium and sulfate ions dries out.

Location Mexico, USA

Color Colorless, white

Luster Sub-glassy to pearly

Hardness 2

Streak White

In some dry climates, gypsum crystals form flowerlike clusters called desert roses.

When the crystal grains are fine, the mineral is known as alabaster, which is easy to carve into statues and sculptures.

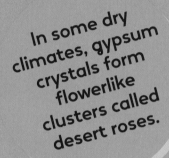

This clear form of gypsum has a typical ram's horn shape.

Cauliflower nodules

What **mineral** is this?

What **streak** does it have?

Where are large **deposits** of it found?

Can it be easily **carved**?

This mineral has a **sub-glassy** appearance. True or false?

It is sometimes **dyed** blue to make it look like what other mineral?

Howlite

This mineral is porous and absorbs dye well, in particular blue dye. When altered in this way, it resembles turquoise. As a result, it is sometimes sold as turquoise. However, it is easily distinguished from turquoise because it is much softer. Large deposits of howlite are found in Death Valley, California.

Location Worldwide

Color White

Luster Sub-glassy

Hardness 3.5

Streak White

Howlite is sometimes found in nodules that look like a cauliflower.

This tumble-polished howlite has been dyed to look like turquoise.

A veined howlite has been used for this frog carving. Howlite is soft but tough, making it an excellent material for carving.

Flat stepped crystals

What **mineral** is this?

What **metal** is it an ore of?

What **sports** equipment can it be used to make?

How is it used in **space** travel?

What **color** is this mineral?

Who was this mineral **named** after?

Ferberite

Ferberite was named in 1863 after the German industrialist and mineralogist Dr. Moritz Rudolph Ferber. It is an iron tungstate that usually occurs as flat, stepped crystals, and is an ore of tungsten. This very useful metal is used in light bulb filaments, sports equipment such as darts and golf clubs, and is also used to harden objects such as drill bits.

Location Japan, Portugal, Romania, South Korea, Rwanda

Color Black, dark brown

Luster Submetallic

Hardness 4–4.5

Streak Black to brown

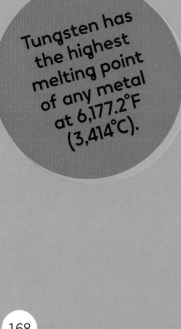

Tungsten has the highest melting point of any metal at 6,177.2°F (3,414°C).

Rocket nozzles, such as those used in Saturn V, are made of heat-resistant, hard, and strong tungsten steel. Saturn V was built to send astronauts to the Moon during the Apollo program.

The deceiver

What **mineral** is this?

This mineral has a **metallic** luster. True or false?

Where in the **world** is it found?

Does it have a **white** streak?

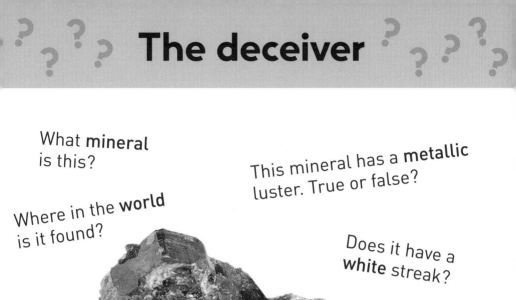

Is it found in a **variety** of colors?

What **Greek** word does it take its name from?

Apatite

The name apatite comes from the Greek *apate*, meaning "deceit," as it often resembles the crystals of other minerals such as aquamarine, amethyst, and peridot. Apatite can be green, blue, violet-blue, purple, colorless, white, yellow, pink, or rose-red. It is used to make many things, including matches.

Location Madagascar, Brazil, Myanmar, Mexico

Color Various

Luster Glassy, waxy

Hardness 5

Streak White

Apatite gems displaying a blue color, such as this one, are among the most popular varieties.

Some of the largest crystals of apatite weigh up to 485 lbs (220 kg).

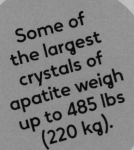

Apatite is found in a number of geological environments, seen here as green crystals within a calcite groundmass.

What **mineral** is this?

What color is it when **freshly** exposed?

Is it **hard** or **soft**?

This mineral is only found in **single** crystals. True or false?

Does is have a **black** streak?

What **pigment** was this mineral the source of?

Vivianite

Vivianite crystals are found singly or in radiating groups. They are colorless when freshly exposed, but then become indigo blue, green, or nearly black. Before the development of modern synthetic chemicals, vivianite was the source of the sought-after blue paint pigment blue ocher.

Location Worldwide

Color Colorless, blue, green, bluish black

Luster Glassy to earthy

Hardness 1.5–2

Streak Bluish white

Vivianite pigment used in paintings becomes bluer when exposed to light.

This vivianite crystal has darkened into a green color.

What **mineral** is this?

Cultures all over the world have used it for many centuries to make beautiful **ornaments**. True or false?

Does this mineral have a **metallic** luster?

What **streak** does it have?

What **Latin** word is it named after?

What **diseases** was this used to treat?

Nephrite

Nephrite is one of two jade minerals; the other is jadeite. Older Chinese jade objects are mostly made from nephrite. The Chinese perfected jade carving in the 1st millennium BCE, and Māori people have been making jade weapons and ornaments for many centuries.

Location Worldwide

Color Translucent white to light yellow

Luster Dull to waxy

Hardness 6.5

Streak White

Nephrite is named after the Latin word nephrus meaning "kidney," because it was once used to treat kidney diseases.

Hei tikis (small neck pendants), such as this one made of nephrite, are worn by the Māori people of New Zealand.

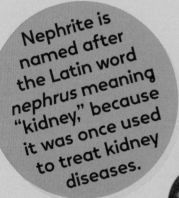

This smiling Buddha was carved from nephrite.

What **mineral** is this?

What **rock** is this mineral a major component of?

It has a pink **streak**. True or false?

Can it be found all over the **world**?

Does it have a **glassy** appearance?

Is it used in making **ceramics**?

Orthoclase

Orthoclase is a major component of granite—its pink crystals give granite its characteristic color. Orthoclase's blocky prismatic crystals can also be white, colorless, cream, pale yellow, or brownish red. This mineral is important in ceramics, where it is used as a clay for making objects and as a glaze.

Location Worldwide

Color Various

Luster Glassy

Hardness 6–6.5

Streak White

Orthoclase can have a shimmering appearance. Mineralogists call this "adularescence."

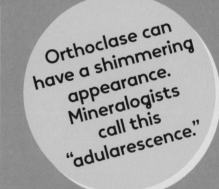

This smooth and shiny variety of orthoclase is a moonstone. It has a silvery shimmer, emphasized by the cut's many facets.

This orthoclase crystal shows the mineral's classic blocky shape in its natural state.

What **mineral** is this?

It is found only in **China**.
True or false?

How many **varieties** of this mineral are there?

What **streak** does this mineral leave?

Can this mineral be **carved**?

It is always **green**.
True or false?

Serpentine

There are at least 16 varieties of serpentine, which is named for its snakeskin-like appearance. Serpentine was carved into vases and bowls on the island of Crete by the Minoans around 3000-1100 BCE. Gem-quality serpentine has a jadelike appearance and is often used in jewelry.

Location Worldwide

Color Various

Luster Sub-glassy to greasy, resinous, earthy, dull

Hardness 3.5–5.5

Streak White

Serpentine can come in many colors, such as this light green piece that has been carved into a seashell.

In folklore, serpentine was used to prevent or cure snakebites.

Mysterious serpentine carvings such as this are found in archaeological sites across northern Britain, and date from about 4,500 years ago.

What **mineral** is this?

Can this mineral have a **greasy** luster?

Where in the **world** is it found?

Does it leave a black **streak**?

What was the first **civilization** to discover and carve this mineral?

What is the most **valuable** color of this mineral?

Jadeite

There are two minerals called jade—nephrite and jadeite. Nephrite comes only in cream and shades of green, while jadeite comes in many other colors, and its pure form is white. The most valuable is emerald green, which is colored by chromium, and known as Imperial Jade.

Location Myanmar, Japan, Guatemala

Color Various

Luster Glassy to greasy

Hardness 6–7

Streak White

The Olmecs were the first of the Mesoamericans (indigenous people of Mexico and Central and South America) to discover and carve jadeite.

Jadeite was incredibly precious to the Mesoamericans. They gave it as a sacred offering to the gods.

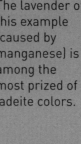

The lavender of this example (caused by manganese) is among the most prized of jadeite colors.

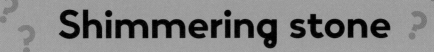

What **mineral** is this?

Is it too **brittle** to be used in jewelry?

It is the **state** gem of Florida.
True or false?

Does it **reflect** light?

Does it always have a **blue** or **white** sheen?

In the past, people used to think it brought **bad luck**. True or false?

Moonstone

Moonstone is so-called because it reflects light to produce the effect of moonlight dancing on water. If you turn a moonstone as you look inside it you will see the same patterns of light that amazed the ancient Romans and Greeks, who once worshipped the stone. Some people believe moonstone has healing properties and brings good luck.

Location Finest found in Sri Lanka and India

Color Colorless, white

Luster Glassy

Hardness 6–6.5

Streak White

Moonstone is the state gem of Florida, from where the Moon landings took off.

This moonstone has a bluish iridescence, which makes the stone glow—moonstone always has a blue or white sheen.

Moonstone has been used in jewelry for centuries. This gold ring is set with a large moonstone, which has a milky white surface.

What **mineral** is this?

Does it have a **metallic** appearance?

Is this a **hard** or **soft** mineral?

This mineral is **warm** to the touch. True or false?

Is it associated with **volcanoes**?

Is this a **rare** element?

Sulfur

Most sulfur forms in volcanic fumaroles, but it can also result from the breakdown of sulfide ore deposits. Massive sulfur is found in thick beds in sedimentary rocks, particularly those associated with salt domes. Sulfur is a poor conductor of heat, which means that specimens are warm to the touch.

Location China, Canada, Germany, Japan

Color Light yellow

Luster Resinous to greasy

Hardness 1.5–2.5

Streak White

Sulfur is the ninth most abundant element in the universe.

Deposits of sulfur occur in fumaroles that formed in 1971 in the Kilauea caldera of Hawai'i.

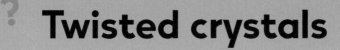

What **mineral** is this?

Does it have a **metallic** appearance?

Where in the **world** is it found?

How was it used in the **ancient** world?

What effect does it have on how **matches** burn?

Is it a useful **ore**?

Stibnite

Stibnite is the main ore of antimony, which is used for hardening lead and is added to paint and plastics as a flame-retardant. Powdered stibnite was used in the ancient world as a cosmetic for eyes to make them look larger.

Location China, Japan, USA

Color Lead-gray to black

Luster Metallic

Hardness 2

Streak Lead gray to steel gray

Ancient Egyptian kohl (a dark eyeshadow) was made from powdered stibnite.

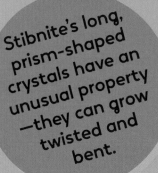

Stibnite's long, prism-shaped crystals have an unusual property —they can grow twisted and bent.

These matches with antimony in the tip burn brighter than ones without it.

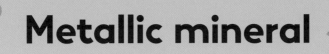

What **mineral** is this?

What **color** is it when freshly exposed?

Why was it associated with **death** in Victorian times?

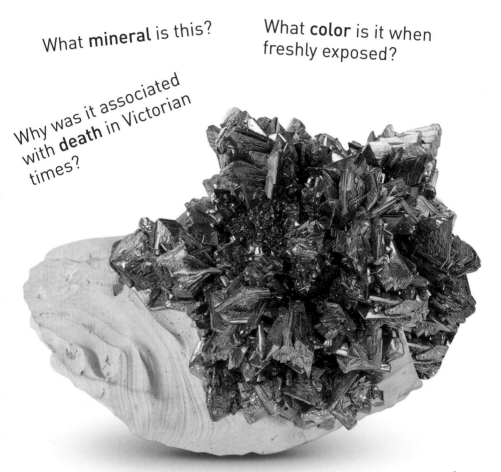

What other **mineral** is it chemically identical to?

Is it found **deep** in the Earth's crust?

Does it have a yellow **streak**?

Marcasite

An iron sulfide, marcasite is chemically identical to pyrite, but unlike pyrite it has an orthorhombic crystal structure. Marcasite is opaque and pale silvery yellow when fresh, but darkens and tarnishes on exposure. It is found near Earth's surface.

Location Worldwide

Color Tin white to bronze yellow

Luster Metallic

Hardness 6–6.5

Streak Gray to black

In late Victorian times, marcasites were widely used for mourning jewelry.

Nodules composed of marcasite crystals come from the chalk deposits of France and England.

Color changer

What **mineral** is this?

Which **emperor** is this mineral named after?

What color is it in **daylight**?

Is the **gemstone** variety of this mineral expensive?

This mineral can also be **red**. True or false?

Is it **hard** or **soft**?

Chrysoberyl

Although crystals of chrysoberyl are common, the gemstone variety alexandrite is one of the rarest and most expensive gems in the world. Alexandrite has the extraordinary visual property of appearing green in daylight but red under incandescent light.

Location Worldwide

Color Green, yellow, brown, red

Luster Glassy

Hardness 8.5

Streak Colorless

Alexandrite was named after the Russian ruler, Alexander II, on whose birthday it was supposedly discovered.

This gold ring from around 1900 features a central stone of cat's-eye chrysoberyl, surrounded by diamonds.

Alexandrite appears greenish in daylight, where a full spectrum of light is present, but reddish in incandescent light because it contains less of the green and blue spectrum.

What **mineral** is this?

It is always a **pink** color. True or false?

Does it look **glassy**?

What color **streak** does this mineral leave?

Can it have **needle-like** crystals?

Where was it first **discovered**?

Diaspore

Diaspore takes its name from the Greek word *diaspora*, which means "scattering"—a reference to the way diaspore crackles under high heat. Its crystals are thin, elongated, tabular, prismatic, or needle-like. The same specimen can appear to have different colors when viewed from different directions.

Location Turkey, Russia, USA

Color White, yellow, lilac, pink

Luster Glassy

Hardness 6.5–7

Streak White

Diaspore displays light green tints in sunlight and raspberry purplish-pinks in candlelight.

This diaspore gemstone has been skilfully faceted.

Diaspore was first discovered in 1801 in the Ural mountains in Russia.

Heavenly color

What **mineral** is this?

Is it always **light blue**?

Does it **break** easily?

Why can't it be **worn** as a gemstone?

Where in the **world** is it found?

What is this mineral an **ore** of?

Celestine

Often light blue in color, celestine takes its name from the Latin word *coelestis*, which means "heavenly"—a reference to the color of the sky. Specimens can also be colorless, white, light red, green, medium to dark blue, or brown. Celestine is an ore of strontium, and is too soft and easily broken to wear.

Location USA, Namibia, Madagascar

Color Colorless, red, green, blue

Luster Glassy, pearly on cleavage

Hardness 3–3.5

Streak White

Massive crystals of celestine measuring more than 30 in (75 cm) have been found.

Celestine is an extremely hard-to-cut collector's gem. This mixed cut shows the very high skill of the cutter.

What **mineral** is this?

It can be formed by some living **animals**. True or false?

Does this mineral have a **glassy** appearance?

Is it **fragile**?

Which **form** of this mineral looks like popcorn?

Why are **groups** of this mineral called sputniks?

Aragonite

Aragonite occurs in rocks in the same way as other minerals, but it is also produced by certain biological processes—the shells of many marine molluscs, as well as corals and pearls, are composed mainly of aragonite. Like all carbonates, it is soft and fragile.

Location Spain, Italy, China

Color Various

Luster Glassy inclining to resinous

Hardness 3.5–4

Streak White

Radiating groups of aragonite are called sputniks or star clusters because of their appearance.

Aragonite sometimes forms in treelike crystal groups. Known as flos ferri, or "popcorn" aragonite, it is brittle and extremely fragile.

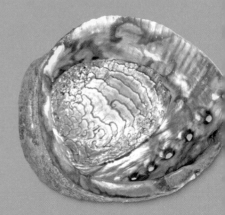

Aragonite is produced by some living animals. It is seen here forming the inner layer of a marine mollusk shell.

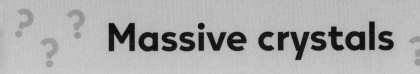

What **mineral** is this?

Does it have a blue **streak**?

How big are the **largest** crystals found of this mineral?

In what **year** was it named?

Is it **hard** or **soft**?

What metal is it an **ore** of?

Anglesite

Named in 1832, anglesite is colorless to white, grayish, yellow, green, or blue, and often fluoresces yellow under ultraviolet light. Exceptionally large crystals—up to 31 in (80 cm) long—have been found. Anglesite has been used since ancient times as an ore of lead.

Location Worldwide

Color Various

Luster Adamantine to resinous, glassy

Hardness 2.5–3

Streak Colorless

Anglesite is soft and easily cleaved. It is one of the stones used to test the skills of master gem cutters.

Anglesite is named after the Welsh island of Anglesey.

This specimen shows a pointed crystal of anglesite.

What **mineral** is this?

Does this mineral have a **metallic** appearance?

What happens when it is **worn** next to the skin?

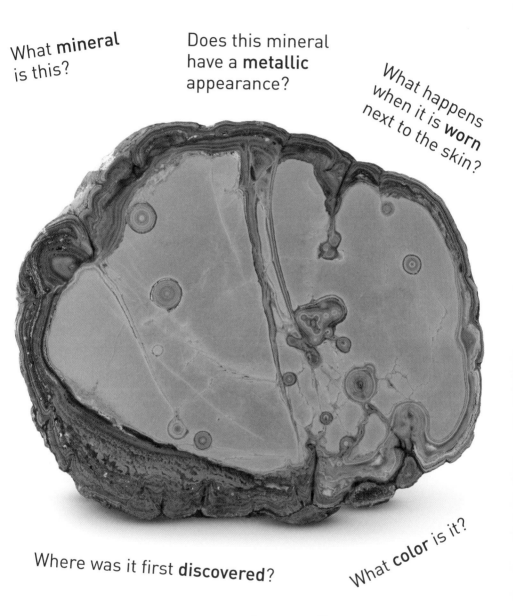

Where was it first **discovered**?

What **color** is it?

Does it have **decorative** uses?

Variscite

This mineral was named after Variscia, the old name for the German district of Voightland, where it was first discovered in 1837. Variscite is pale to apple green in color. It is valued as a semiprecious gemstone, and is used for carvings and as a decorative material.

Location Austria, Czech Republic, Australia, Venezuela, USA

Color Pale to apple-green

Luster Glassy to waxy

Hardness 4.5

Streak White

Variscite that is unsuitable as a gemstone is often tumble polished to show the interesting swirls and patterns and sold for decorative use.

When worn next to the skin, variscite absorbs body oils, which discolor it.

Variscite can be polished into inexpensive gems, but their softness makes them vulnerable to wear.

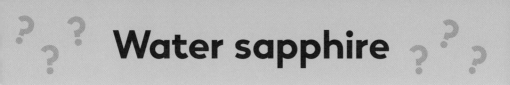

What **mineral** is this?

Does it have a white **streak**?

What is it called when it is **gem-quality**?

Which **car** part is this mineral found in?

Does it always look **blue**?

Where in the **world** is it found?

Cordierite

Gem-quality blue cordierite is known as iolite, derived from a Greek word meaning "violet," a reference to its color. As a gemstone, its color changes, appearing intense blue in one direction, yellowish gray or blue in another, and almost colorless as the stone is turned in the third direction.

Location Worldwide

Color Various

Luster Glassy to greasy

Hardness 7–7.5

Streak White

Cordierite is used to produce the ceramics inside catalytic converters in cars.

These flower earrings feature a central iolite, with pink tourmalines forming the "petals."

The sapphire blue color of iolite shows why it is also known as water sapphire.

Rich blue-green

What **mineral** is this?

This mineral is found all over the **world**. True or false?

The name of this mineral is derived from which two **Greek** words?

Does this mineral have a **dull** appearance?

Is it prized as a **gemstone**?

Who **first** used the name of this mineral in 315 BCE?

Chrysocolla

The term chrysocolla was first used by the Greek philosopher Theophrastus in 315 BCE to refer to various materials used in soldering gold. The name is derived from two Greek words: *chrysos*, which means "gold," and *kolla*, which means "glue."

Location Worldwide

Color Blue, blue-green

Luster Glassy to earthy

Hardness 2–4

Streak Pale blue, tan, gray

This bird resting on a cluster of berries has been carved from chrysocolla.

Rich blue-green chrysocolla, such as the stone in this bracelet, is highly prized as a gemstone.

Theophrastus was the first scholar to attempt a systematic classification of gems and minerals.

What **mineral** is this?

This mineral has a blue **streak**. True or false?

Is it **glassy** or **metallic** looking?

Which sapphire-blue **gemstone** is mined from this mineral?

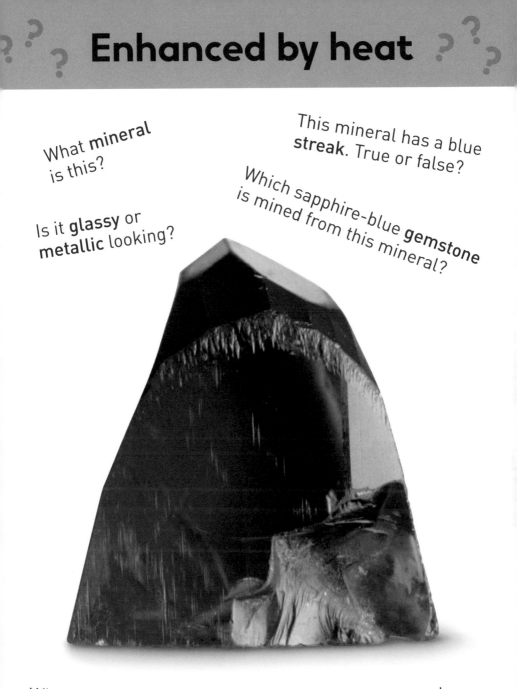

What is the name of the **pink variety** of this mineral that is found in Norway?

Is this mineral only **found** in Norway?

Orthorhombic
Silicates

Zoisite

Although best known for its sapphire-blue gemstone called tanzanite, there are other gemstone varieties. A pink variety found in Norway is called thulite and is named after Thule, which is an old name for the country. Zoisite can also be green, yellowish green, green-brown, white, colorless, or gray.

Location Worldwide

Color Various

Luster Glassy

Hardness 6–7

Streak White

This piece of light pink rough thulite would be suitable for carving, or used as a gemstone.

Anyolite, a brilliant green variety of zoisite sprinkled with rubies, is popular as a carving and ornamental stone.

Tanzanite gems over 5 carats are uncommon. This triangular brilliant-cut gem weighs 15.34 carats.

Emerald imitator

What **mineral** is this?

What is the name of the **gemstone** mined from this mineral?

This mineral is only found in one **country**. True or false?

What determines its shade and depth of **color**?

Does this mineral have a **pearly** appearance?

Where in Istanbul's Topkapi Palace would you **find** it?

Olivine

Olivine refers to a group of silicate minerals that form in molten rock beneath Earth's surface. The ancient Greeks and Romans were among the first people to use these minerals for decoration. Peridot is the gem-quality variety of olivine.

Location Worldwide

Color Yellow to yellow-green

Luster Glassy

Hardness 6.5–7

Streak White

The gold throne in the Topkapi Palace collection in Istanbul, Turkey, is decorated with 955 peridots.

The proportion of iron present determines the shade and depth of color. The light green color of this peridot shows a low concentration of iron.

This pendant features a flawless peridot.

What **mineral** is this?

Which island in the **Red Sea** gives this mineral its name?

Is it **hard** or **soft**?

What color **streak** does it have?

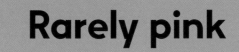

Is this mineral found in any **other** colors?

How is the color of this mineral made **darker**?

Topaz

In the past, many yellowish gems, such as peridot and garnets, were called topaz. The gem was used in ancient Egypt, Greece, and Rome. The earliest source of topaz was an island in the Red Sea called Zabargad, which was known as Topazios in ancient times. However, it is thought the gems found there were actually peridot.

Location Worldwide

Color Various

Luster Glassy

Hardness 8

Streak Colorless

A rare natural pink topaz was used in this gold ring.

Ancient Egyptians believed the sun god Ra gave topaz a golden glow.

Blue topaz is made darker by exposing it to radiation.

What **mineral** is this?

What are the most **prized** colors for its gemstones?

Is this mineral used to make **glass**?

Does this mineral have a **silky** or **glassy** appearance?

Is this mineral **only** used as a gemstone?

Does it have a purple or white **streak**?

Sillimanite

Although mainly an industrial material, transparent sillimanite is the basis of attractive gemstones. They are cut from a form of sillimanite called fibrolite, so named because the mineral resembles bunches of fibers twisted together. Blue and violet are the most prized colors for gemstones.

Location Worldwide

Color Colorless, blue, yellow, green, violet

Luster Silky

Hardness 7

Streak White

Sillimanite is pleochroic: yellowish-green, dark green, and blue can be seen within the same stone from different angles.

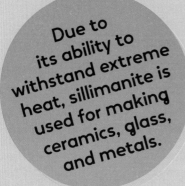

Due to its ability to withstand extreme heat, sillimanite is used for making ceramics, glass, and metals.

This is a rare example of a gem-quality fibrous sillimanite.

Ancient gem

What **mineral** is this?

Does it have a **metallic** appearance?

When were the earliest **objects** from this mineral made?

The **finest** examples of this mineral are mined in which country?

How is this mineral thought to bring good **luck**?

What causes it to be different **colors**?

Turquoise

Beads made from turquoise dating back to c.5000 BCE have been found in Mesopotamia (present-day Iraq), making it one of the first gems to be mined and cut. Turquoise varies in color from sky-blue to green, depending on the amount of iron and copper it contains.

Location Worldwide

Color Blue, green

Luster Waxy to dull

Hardness 5–6

Streak White to green

In Persia (modern-day Iran), seeing the reflection of a New Moon on a turquoise stone symbolized good luck.

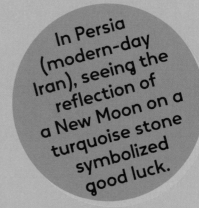

Turquoise from Nishapur, Iran (formerly Persia), is considered by many to be the finest quality and has been mined for centuries.

This Chinese carving of an elephant has been crafted from turquoise.

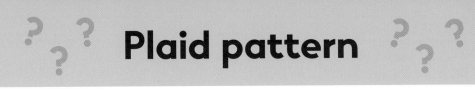

What **mineral** is this?

Is this mineral **glassy** or **metallic** looking?

How **large** can its crystals be?

What are blue-green to green specimens of this mineral **called**?

How is it **used**?

Is it **mined** in Brazil?

Microcline

Used in ceramics and as a mild abrasive, microcline forms short prismatic or tabular crystals that are often of considerable size: single crystals can weigh several tons, and reach meters in length. Crystals are often twinned. This gives a "plaid" effect that is unique to microcline among the feldspars.

Location Russia, USA, Brazil

Color Various

Luster Glassy, dull

Hardness 6–6.5

Streak White

Blue-green to green specimens of microcline are called amazonstone or amazonite.

The name microcline originates from the Greek for "small slope."

Gem-quality amazonite is found in Minas Gerais in Brazil, Colorado in the USA, and the Ural Mountains in Russia.

Rock-forming

What **mineral** is this?

Does it have a white or purple **streak**?

Where in the **world** is it found?

Is it found as **well-formed** crystals?

What **material** does it form when mixed with clay?

It is used in **jewelry**. True or false?

Albite

Albite is mainly significant as a rock-forming mineral, but it also has some use as a gemstone. It is found as well-formed and glassy crystals, and these are often of transparent gem quality. However, it is relatively soft and brittle.

Location Canada, Brazil, Norway

Color White, colorless, yellow, green

Luster Glassy to pearly

Hardness 6–6.5

Streak White

Although fragile, albite is sometimes used in jewelry, along with albite's moonstone variety.

When mixed with clay, albite forms porcelain that is tough but delicate-looking.

In this specimen, tourmaline and quartz crystals rest on albite.

What **mineral** is this?

Can it form **twinned** crystals?

This mineral is bright **red**. True or false?

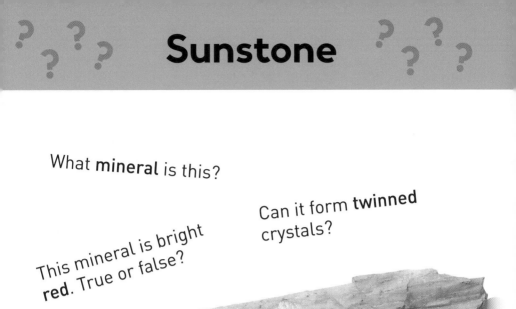

Does it have a **pearly** appearance?

What **rocks** can this mineral occur in?

What **Greek** words give this mineral its name?

Oligoclase

Oligoclase can be gray, white, red, greenish, yellowish, brown, or colorless. Its usual habit is massive or granular, although it can form tabular crystals that are often twinned. Oligoclase occurs in feldspar- and quartz-rich igneous rocks. It also occurs in high-grade, metamorphosed gneisses and schists.

Location Worldwide

Color Various

Luster Glassy

Hardness 6

Streak White

Oligoclase gets its name from the Greek words oligos, which means "little," and clasein, "to break."

This gold pin with an oligoclase sunstone shows off the gemstone's internal sparkles.

This is an uncut sample of oligoclase sunstone.

What **mineral** is this?

Does it have a blue **streak**?

This mineral displays many **colors**. True or false?

Is it used in **jewelry**?

What country produces a **rare** variety of this mineral?

What is the **iridescence** in this mineral called?

Labradorite

Gemstone labradorite is characterized by its iridescent colors. Crystals that display this effect are used for jewelry or carvings. Labradorite is generally blue or dark gray, but can also be colorless or white. When transparent, labradorite is yellow, red, orange, or green.

Location Worldwide

Color Blue, gray, white

Luster Glassy

Hardness 6–6.5

Streak White

The polished oval of labradorite in this piece of jewelry displays the stone's rainbow iridescence.

The iridescence in labradorite is called schiller. This square-cut labradorite has fine blue, gold, and green schiller.

Spectrolite, a rare variety from Finland, displays a more dazzling range of iridescent colors than other labradorites.

Powdery mineral

What **mineral** is this?

Why is it added to **paint**?

Can it be **carved**?

What **rock** is it the main ingredient of?

It is only found in one **country**. True or false?

Does it **crumble** easily?

Talc

One of Earth's softest minerals, talc is ground finely to make talcum powder. It is the main ingredient of soapstone, and has traditionally been carved to make ornaments. Talc is also used in paints and for making paper. It is found in most areas of the world.

Location Worldwide

Color Whitish gray to green

Luster Pearly to greasy

Hardness 1

Streak White

Soapstone, such as that used in this Chinese seal, has been used to carve ornaments for thousands of years.

Apart from flint, soapstone may be the first rock that humans cut or engraved.

Smooth, powdered talc adds thickness to paint.

Lipstick sheen

What **mineral** is this?

Is this mineral **glassy** looking?

What happens when it is **heated**?

Why is it added to **lipstick**?

Is it **hard** or **soft**?

Where does its **name** come from?

Pyrophyllite

The name of this mineral is based on the Greek words for "fire" and "leaf" because it sheds thin, leaf-like layers when heated. It provides a sheen to lipsticks and is also used as a filler in paints and rubber. Ancient cultures used it to carve small objects.

Location Worldwide

Color Various

Luster Pearly to dull

Hardness 1–2

Streak White

This simple pendant, dating between the 4th and 8th century, was discovered in Costa Rica.

Bright, reflective flakes of powdered pyrophyllite are added to lipstick to give it a high sheen.

Pyrophyllite is often so fine-grained that it appears textureless.

Rosy hues

What **mineral** is this?

Does it have a **white** or **pink** streak?

What is this mineral a **source** of?

Is it **widespread** or **rare**?

What Greek word does it take its **name** from?

Is it mined as a **gem**?

Rhodonite

Rhodonite takes its name from the Greek *rhodon*, meaning "rose." It is a source of manganese, and is widespread, but it is usually mined as a semiprecious gem and ornamental stone. It is typically a pink color. However, material streaked with black veins is also favored by carvers and cutters.

Location Worldwide

Color Pink to rose-red

Luster Glassy

Hardness 6

Streak White

The manganese in rhodonite turns black when exposed to the air.

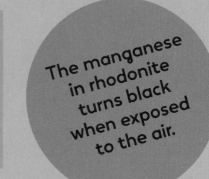

This rhodonite carving of a bear catching a salmon was created in a German gem-cutting center.

This spectacular decorative box has been carved from rhodonite that is black-streaked and has layers of quartz.

Ax-shaped crystals

What **mineral** is this?

How **many** minerals are in this group?

What is the most common **color** for this mineral?

This mineral can have **blocky** crystals. True or false?

What happens when it is rapidly **heated** or **cooled**?

Is this mineral **dull** looking?

Triclinic
Silicates

Axinite

Axinite refers to a group of four minerals, which in their rough form are structurally identical. The name derives from the Greek *axine*, meaning "ax," which describes the sharp, hard crystals. The most common color is brown, but varieties can also be gray to bluish gray, pink, violet-blue, yellow, or red.

Location Worldwide

Color Brown, gray, pink, violet, yellow, red

Luster Glassy

Hardness 6.5–7

Streak Colorless to light brown

Although axinite is often found as thin, hard, ax-head-shaped crystals, it can also be found in blocky form, as shown here.

Axinite generates electricity when stressed, or rapidly heated or cooled.

This axinite crystal is an unusual shade of violet, popular with collectors.

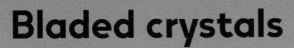

What **mineral** is this?

Where are **gem-quality** crystals mined?

What **car part** is it used to make?

Is this mineral found in more than one **color** form?

What was this mineral previously **called**?

It has a blue **streak**. True or false?

Kyanite

This silicate has been used to make heat-resistant porcelains, such as those used in sparkplugs. Gem-quality kyanite crystals are found in Bahia, Brazil. Its name is taken from the Greek word *kyanos*, meaning "dark blue"—a reference to one of its many color forms.

Location Brazil, Switzerland, USA

Color Blue, green, orange, colorless

Luster Glassy

Hardness 4.5–6

Streak Colorless

These earrings are set with blue kyanite stones.

Kyanite's former name, disthene, means "two strengths" as its hardness varies within the same crystal.

Kyanite is mined for the aluminum silicate mullite, which is used in sparkplugs.

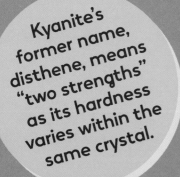

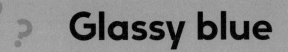

What **mineral** is this?

It **dissolves** easily in water. True or false?

What **metal** is this mineral an ore of?

What was the old **name** for this mineral?

Is it common in countries that get a lot of **rain**?

Is this mineral **hard** or **soft**?

Chalcanthite

Chalcanthite dissolves easily in water and is therefore more common in dry regions. It used to be known as blue vitriol, but takes its name from the Greek words *khalkos*, which means "copper," and *anthos*, which means "flower." It is an important ore of copper, especially in dry countries such as Chile.

Location Chile, USA

Color Bright blue, sky-blue, greenish-blue

Luster Glassy

Hardness 2.5

Streak Colorless

Chalcanthite is toxic to humans, as it can cause copper poisoning.

This stalactite of the mineral chalcanthite was formed from copper-rich waters in a mine.

This section of a mine shows the roof colored with deposits of chalcanthite.

Skeletal material

What **mineral** is this?

Which female monster's blood formed this mineral, according to Greek **legend**?

Is this mineral **soft** or **hard**?

Which marine **animals** make this mineral?

Does it have a **metallic** appearance?

What substance forms **black** and **golden** versions of this mineral?

Coral

According to Greek legend, coral came from the drops of blood shed when Perseus slayed the monster Medusa. Coral is actually the skeletal material made by marine animals known as coral polyps. In most corals, this material is calcium carbonate, but in black and golden corals it is a hornlike substance called conchiolin.

Location Worldwide

Color Various

Luster Dull to glassy

Hardness 3.5

Streak White

The Greek word for coral is *georgia*, named after the mythical gorgons, one of which was Medusa.

Coral is associated with the safeguarding of children, and this miniature carving may have been a gift intended to bring protection to the wearer.

This coral cross-section shows the banded structure of the material. The luster is dull when harvested, but polishing makes it shine.

Hidden gem

What **mineral** is this?

Is it **pearly** or **metallic** looking?

How is it **formed**?

Where is it **found**?

Is it **hard** or **soft**?

What causes the **sheen** on this mineral?

Pearl

Pearls are one of the most desirable organic minerals. Made inside the shells of mollusks, they grow in layers around a small piece of sand or foreign particle. Natural pearls that form in the wild are rare, and therefore valuable, and pearl divers have to open hundreds of pearl oysters before finding one.

Location Worldwide (seas)

Color Various

Luster Pearly

Hardness 3

Streak White

These cultivated pearls show the color variations possible depending on the growth environment.

In Japan, pearl diving without breathing equipment has been a tradition for 2,000 years.

The sheen on pearls and some shells is caused by light reflecting on tiny platelets of calcium called nacre.

238

What **mineral** is this?

The only use of this mineral is in **jewelry**. True or false?

Does this mineral have a **white** or **black** streak?

Which **mollusk** provides some of the most beautiful examples of this mineral?

Where can this mineral be **found**?

Shell

Some of the most beautiful mother-of-pearl comes from the shell of a mollusk called an abalone, with its silvery layers and iridescent multicolored interior. As well as jewelry, mother-of-pearl from giant oysters is used for human bone implants.

Location Worldwide

Color Various

Luster Dull to glassy

Hardness 2.5

Streak White

This magnificent pitcher is made from nautilus shells.

Adult conch shells can grow up to 12 in (30 cm) in size. The shells were once used to make tools and wind instruments.

Throughout history, shells have been used as currency by different cultures.

Trapped sunlight

What **mineral** is this?

In which **palace** in Russia can you find a room lavishly decorated with this mineral?

Does it have a **yellow** or **white** streak?

It can be found on the **seafloor**. True or false?

How is it **formed**?

How can this mineral be **distinguished** from fakes?

Amber

According to the ancient Greeks, this substance contained trapped sunlight. Like preserved pollen or a pinecone, amber is part of an ancient tree that lived millions of years ago. It forms from hardened resin that oozes from inside a tree. Amber can also be found on the seafloor.

Location Eastern Europe, Dominican Republic, USA

Color Golden-yellow

Luster Resinous

Hardness 2–2.5

Streak White

As resin dried 40–50 million years ago, insects were sometimes fossilized within the sticky substance.

When rubbed, amber gives a static charge. This helps experts to spot a fake.

This room in the Catherine Palace in St. Petersburg, Russia, is a recreation of the original amber-laden room, which was destroyed in World War II.

What **mineral** is this?

Is it **metallic** looking?

Can it be **mined**?

Where in the **world** is it found?

What **Aztec** word is it named after?

It can be collected from a **living organism**. True or false?

Copal

Copal is named after the word *copalli* from the Aztec language. It means "resin." Copal is a yellow to red-orange resin obtained from various tropical trees. It can be collected from living trees, and from the soil beneath the trees. It can also be mined if it is buried.

Location China, Tanzania, South America

Color Yellow to red-orange

Luster Resinous

Hardness 2–2.5

Streak White

For centuries, copal has been burned as incense in Mesoamerica as an offering to the Mayan gods.

The flattened, globular shape of this example of copal is the result of its original resin forming a pool on the forest floor.

This group of gemmy copal pieces shows a variety of different shades and colors.

Solid fuel

What **mineral** is this?

What color **streak** does it have?

Is it **hard** or **soft**?

How is this mineral **formed**?

What are the four **varieties** of this mineral?

Coal

Coal is formed from the fossilized remains of plants. Different varieties of coal are formed, depending on the plant material, coalification (the process by which plant material is converted to coal), and the presence of impurities. There are four varieties: lignite, anthracite, sub-bituminous coal, and bituminous coal.

Location Worldwide

Color Brown, black

Luster Nearly metallic

Hardness 2–2.5

Streak Black

This piece of anthracite is polished to a sheen, showing how it can sometimes be used as a jet substitute.

The deeper coal is buried, the denser and more energy-rich it is.

Shown here are samples of bituminous coal (ordinary household coal) and anthracite.

What **mineral** is this?

The color of this mineral **fades** quickly. True or false?

Does it have a **metallic** appearance?

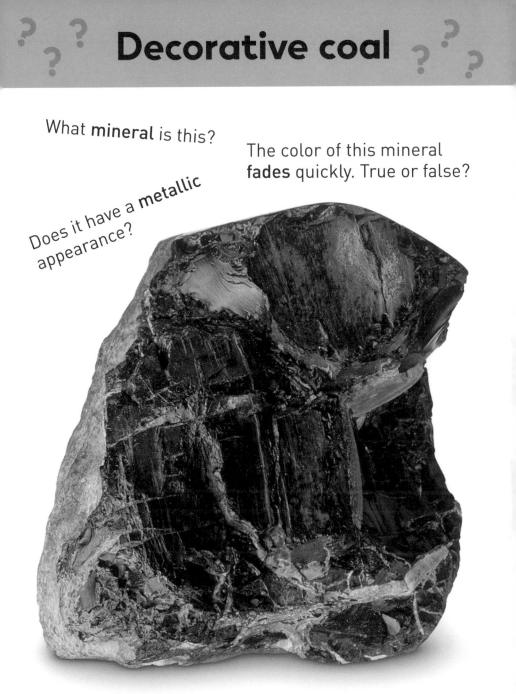

How was it used by the **Romans**?

What **color** is it?

How is it **classified**?

Jet

Classified as a type of coal, jet has been carved for decorative purposes since prehistoric times. The Romans carved jet into bangles and beads. In medieval Europe, powdered jet drunk with water or wine was believed to have medicinal properties.

Location Worldwide

Color Dark brown, black

Luster Velvety, glassy, or waxy

Hardness 2.5

Streak Black to dark brown

Many Indigenous nations, such as the Hopi and Zuni, use jet to create jewelry. This spectacular jet eagle also has turquoise stones.

The color of this mineral never fades, and its polished surface can be used as a mirror.

Gemstone fossil

What **mineral** is this?

Does it have a **glassy** appearance?

Where are the best examples of this mineral **mined**?

This mineral is formed from fossil shells of **ammonites**. True or false?

What are the most **common colors** of this mineral?

Ammolite

Ammolite is the lining of the fossil shells of ammonites—sea animals that were related to today's squid and octopuses. Its iridescent colors cross the spectrum, but green and red are most common, with gold or purple being rarer. It is found in many parts of the world, but the best examples come from Alberta, Canada, where it is mined.

Location Best examples come from Alberta, Canada

Color All spectral colors

Luster Glassy

Hardness 3.5–4

Streak Colorless

Ammonites became extinct about 66 million years ago, around the same time as the non-avian dinosaurs.

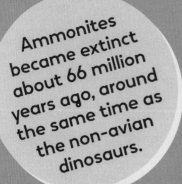

Shown here is a section of the fossilized outer shell of an ammonite, revealing the colors that makes this material desirable.

This fossil ammonite has been sawed and polished to reveal its inner chambers, infilled with calcite.

Glossary

Adamantine luster
A type of bright mineral luster similar to that of diamond.

Alloy
A metallic material, such as brass, bronze, or steel, that is a mixture of two types of metal.

Brilliant cut
A round cut featuring numerous facets designed to maximize a gemstone's brilliance.

Crystal
A solid with an ordered internal atomic structure that produces a typical external shape, along with characteristic physical and optical properties.

Detrital
A type of sediment that has settled in water or has been deposited by water.

Extrusive rock
An igneous rock that formed from magma that solidified above ground.

Facet
A flat face cut into a gemstone. A cut stone is called faceted.

Feldspars
A group of 16 silicate or aluminosilicate minerals. The most important contain calcium or sodium (plagioclase) or potassium (potassium feldspar) and are major constituents of rocks.

Fluorescence
The optical effect whereby a mineral appears to glow in ultraviolet (UV) light. It often glows a different color under UV light than it does in ordinary light.

Fossil
A trace of past life that has been preserved in a rock or mineral such as amber. Fossils include bones, shells, skin impressions, footprints, dung, wood, leaves, and pollen.

Gemstone
A high-quality, hard mineral, which is valued for its color and rarity.

Geode
A cavity in a rock that has been filled, or partially filled, with crystals. It is sometimes called a "thunder egg".

Groundmass
The compact, fine-grained mineral material in which larger crystals or grains are embedded.

Habit
The general appearance and shape of a mineral. A mineral's habit can be affected by its crystal system and the conditions under which it grew.

Intrusive rock
An igneous rock that forms when magma solidifies below the surface.

Iridescence
The reflection of light from the internal elements of a stone, yielding a rainbow-like play of colors.

Lava
Magma that has erupted at Earth's surface.

Mafic rock
Igneous rock that contains between 45 percent and 55 percent total silica. These have less than 10 percent quartz and are rich in ferro-magnesian minerals.

Magma
Molten rock created in the upper mantle, deep below the surface of Earth.

Massive
A term used to describe a mineral that has no definite shape.

Matrix
Also known as groundmass, the matrix of a rock is the fine-grained mass in which larger grains or crystals are embedded.

Meteorite
A rock or dusty debris from outer space that reaches the surface of Earth.

Mica
Any of a group of hydrous potassium or aluminium silicate minerals. These minerals exhibit a two-dimensional sheet- or layer-like structure.

Mohs scale
The measure of a gem's relative hardness based on its resistance to scratching.

Moonstone
A gem-quality feldspar mineral that exhibits a silvery or bluish iridescence. Several feldspars, especially some plagioclases, are called moonstone.

Nacre
Also called mother-of-pearl, a coating produced by shellfish, which forms the shiny coating of a pearl.

Nodule
A hard, rounded, stony lump found in sedimentary rock. It is typically made from calcite, silica, pyrite, or gypsum.

Nugget
A small lump of a precious metal found in its native state.

Ore
A rock or mineral from which a metal can be profitably extracted.

Organic gem
A gem that is composed of material made by, or from, living organisms.

Pegmatite
A hydrothermal vein composed of large crystals.

Pigment
A colored substance that is powdered and mixed to make paint.

Pleochroic
The phenomenon of a mineral or gem presenting different colors to the eye when viewed from different directions.

Pluton
Any body of intrusive igneous rock.

Prismatic
Crystals with a uniform cross-section, having parallel long sides.

Resinous luster
A luster with the reflectivity of resin.

Schiller
The brilliant play of bright colors in a crystal, often due to minute, rod-like inclusions.

Sediment
Particles of rock, mineral, or organic matter that are carried by wind, water, and ice.

Stalactite
A hanging spike made of calcium carbonate (lime) formed as dripping water precipitates lime from the roof of a cave. Over a long period of time, stony stalactites build up in size and may hang many yards from a cave roof.

Sunstone
A gemstone variety of feldspar with minute, plate-like inclusions of iron oxide orientated parallel to one another throughout.

Tabular
A habit in which crystals take the shape of a thin box.

Tetrahedral
A crystal made up of four triangular faces in pairs, rotated 90 degrees from each other.

Translucent
A substance that allows light to pass through it.

Twinned crystals
Crystals that grow together as mirror images with a common face or at angles of up to 90 degrees to each other.

Index

255

Acknowledgments

For Smithsonian Enterprises
Avery Naughton, Licensing Coordinator; Paige Towler,
Editorial Lead; Jill Corcoran, Senior Director, Licensed Publishing;
Brigid Ferraro, Vice President of New Business and Licensing;
Carol LeBlanc, President

The publisher would like to thank the following for their kind permission
to reproduce their photographs:
(Key: a-above; b-below/bottom; c-center; f-far; l-left; r-right; t-top)

1 Dorling Kindersley: Holts Gems. 7 Science Photo Library: Richard Bizley.
11 Dreamstime.com: Helena Bilkova (b); Natthaphong Janpum (t). Getty
Images: Kevin Schafer (c). 12 Dreamstime.com: Dmitry Pichugin. 14
Dorling Kindersley: Natural History Museum, London (cr). 15 Dorling
Kindersley: Holts Gems, Hatton Garden (b). 16 Dorling Kindersley: Holts
Gems (t, c, cb). Dreamstime.com: Mohamed El-Jaouhari (b). 17 Dorling
Kindersley: Oxford University Museum of Natural History (b). 18
Dreamstime.com: Cristian M. Vela (c/Amber). 22 Dorling Kindersley:
Natural History Museum, London (crb/Pegmatite B). 26 Dreamstime.com:
Gorodok495-SDEL0- (crb). 28 Alamy Stock Photo: funkyfood London -
Paul Williams (br/Porphyry B). Shutterstock.com: FlatlandPic (clb/Porphyry
B). 30 Dreamstime.com: Rafal Kubiak (crb/Basalt B); Saiko3p (bl/Basalt
B). 32 123RF.com: dmitryst (bl/Kimberlite B). Shutterstock.com: Damian
Ryszawy (crb/Kimberlite B). 33 Dorling Kindersley: Science Museum,
London (Pumice). 34 Dreamstime.com: Frederic Prochasson (Pumice B).
36 Dorling Kindersley: Michel Zabe / CONACULTA-INAH-MEX (b/Obsidian
B). 38 Dorling Kindersley: Holts Gems (crb/Anorthosite B, br/Anorthosite
B). 40 Dreamstime.com: Vichaya Kiatyingangsulee (Dolerite B). 42 Alamy
Stock Photo: Phil Degginger (Gneiss B). 44 Dorling Kindersley: University
of Aberdeen (bl/Schist B). Getty Images / iStock: geogif (crb/Schist B).
46 Dorling Kindersley: Blists Hill and Jackfield Tile Museum, Ironbridge,
Shropshire (clb/Slate B). Dreamstime.com: Mitchell Barutha (br/Slate B).
49 Dreamstime.com: Annausova75 (Soapstone). 50 Dorling Kindersley:
University of Pennsylvania Museum of Archaeology and Anthropology (crb/
Soapstone B). 52 Dreamstime.com: Arenaphotouk (clb/Marble B). 54
Dorling Kindersley: Peter Harper / © The Trustees of the British Museum.
All rights reserved. 56 Dreamstime.com: Luckyphotographer (br/
Sandstone B). 60 Dorling Kindersley: Natural History Museum, London
(clb/Mudstone B). 62 Dreamstime.com: R2d2v1 (br/Graywacke B). 64
Dorling Kindersley: University of Pennsylvania Museum of Archaeology
and Anthropology (Limestone B). 66 Getty Images / iStock: AlexKosev
(br/Chalk B). 69 Dorling Kindersley: Natural History Museum, London
(Copper). 70 Dreamstime.com: Dibrova (br/Copper B). 71 Dorling
Kindersley: Natural History Museum, London (Platinum). 72 Alamy Stock
Photo: icollection (br/Platinum B); Friedrich Saurer (bl/Platinum B).
74 Dorling Kindersley: RGB Research Limited (clb/Iron B). Science Photo
Library: Jim West (br/Iron B). 76 Dreamstime.com: Michal Janoek (Gold B).
79 Dorling Kindersley: Oxford University Museum of Natural History
(Diamond). 80 Courtesy of Smithsonian. ©2020 Smithsonian: Chip Clark
(clb/Diamond B). Dorling Kindersley: Natural History Museum, London
(br/Diamond B). 83 Dreamstime.com: Vvoevale (Pyrite). 84 Dorling
Kindersley: Oxford University Museum of Natural History (br/Pyrite B).
86 Alamy Stock Photo: Lordprice Collection (Uraninite B). 88 Dorling
Kindersley: Oxford University Museum of Natural History (bl/Cuprite B).
90 Alamy Stock Photo: Thomas Schneider / imageBROKER (br/Chromite
B). Dorling Kindersley: RGB Research Limited (clb/Chromite B). 92 Dorling
Kindersley: Holts Gems (bl/Fluorite B). Dreamstime.com: Bogdan Dumitru
(clb/Fluorite B). 94 123RF.com: Francis Dean (br/Halite B). 95
Dreamstime.com: Mohamed El-Jaouhari (Sylvite). 96 Dreamstime.com:
Lightfieldstudiosprod (Sylvite B). 100 Dorling Kindersley: Holts Gems (bl/
Sodalite B). 102 Dorling Kindersley: Oxford University Museum of Natural
History (clb/Chalcopyrite B). 106 Dorling Kindersley: Natural History
Museum, London (clb/Cassiterite B). 108 Dorling Kindersley: Natural
History Museum, London (bl/Scheelite B). 112 Dorling Kindersley: Holts
Gems (crb/Zircon B, bl/Zircon B). 120 Courtesy of Smithsonian. ©2020
Smithsonian: Chip Clark (Millerite B). 122 Dorling Kindersley: Llandrindod
Wells National Cycle (clb/Molybdenite B). Science Photo Library: (br/
Molybdenite B). 125 Dorling Kindersley: Natural History Museum, London
(Proustite). 127 Alamy Stock Photo: Patrick Endres / Alaska Stock / Design
Pics Inc (Ice). 128 Dreamstime.com: Rita Jayaraman (clb/Ice B); Porbital
(br/Ice B). 129 Dorling Kindersley: Holts Gems (Corundum). 130 Courtesy
of Smithsonian. ©2020 Smithsonian: Chip Clark (br/Corundum B). 132
Dorling Kindersley: Tim Parmenter / Natural History Museum, London
(crb). Getty Images / iStock: wanderluster (br). 134 Shutterstock.com: Erik
Pendzich (Calcite B). 136 Alamy Stock Photo: PjrRocks (br/Smithsonite B).
138 123RF.com: Chaiyaphong Kitphaephaisan / winnieapple (r). 140
123RF.com: Mykola Davydenko (br/Vanadinite B); kaetana (bl/Vanadinite

B). 142 Getty Images: Siede Preis / Photodisc (bl/Quartz B). 143 Dorling
Kindersley: Holts Gems (Beryl). 145 Dorling Kindersley: Ruth Jenkinson /
Holts Gems. 146 Dorling Kindersley: Colin Keates / Natural History
Museum, London. 147 Dorling Kindersley: Richard Leeney / Holts Gems,
Hatton Garden. 148 Dorling Kindersley: Tim Parmenter / Natural History
Museum, London (crb); Dorling Kindersley: Ruth Jenkinson / Holts Gems
(b). 149 Dorling Kindersley: Ruth Jenkinson / Holts Gems. 150 Dorling
Kindersley: Tim Parmenter / Natural History Museum, London (crb). 151
Dorling Kindersley: Gary Ombler, Oxford University Museum of Natural
History (l). 152 Dorling Kindersley: Tim Parmenter / Natural History
Museum (bl). 154 123RF.com: Maksym Yemelyanov (cb/Realgar B).
Dorling Kindersley: Natural History Museum, London (bc/Realgar B). 155
Dorling Kindersley: Oxford University Museum of Natural History (Cryolite).
156 PunchStock: Rainer Dittrich / Westend61 (Cryolite B). 158 Dorling
Kindersley: Natural History Museum, London (clb/Azurite B). 160 Dorling
Kindersley: Natural History Museum, London (bl/Malachite B).
Dreamstime.com: Gator (br/Malachite B). 162 Dreamstime.com:
Supertrooper (cb/Colemanite B). Shutterstock.com: Brad Ju (br/
Colemanite B). 164 Dreamstime.com: Thvietz (clb/Gypsum B). Science
Photo Library: Dirk Wiersma (br/Gypsum B). 166 Dorling Kindersley: Holts
Gems, Hatton Garden (br/Howlite B); Natural History Museum, London (bl/
Howlite B). 168 Alamy Stock Photo: p.portal.photo (Ferberite B). 170
Dorling Kindersley: Holts Gems (crb/Apatite B). 171 Dorling Kindersley:
Oxford University Museum of Natural History (Vivianite). 172 Dreamstime.
com: Ruslan Minakryn (Vivianite B). 173 Dreamstime.com: Ruslan
Minakryn (Nephrite). 174 Dorling Kindersley: Holts Gems, Hatton Garden
(bl/Nephrite B); Natural History Museum, London (br/Nephrite B). 176
Dorling Kindersley: Natural History Museum, London (br/Orthoclase B, bl/
Orthoclase B). 177 Dorling Kindersley: Colin Keates / Natural History
Museum, London. 178 Dorling Kindersley: Holts Gems (clb/Serpentine B);
University of Aberdeen (br/Serpentine B). 180 Dorling Kindersley: Natural
History Museum, London (bl/Jadeite B). Getty Images: Universal History
Archive (br/Jadeite B). 181 Dorling Kindersley: Colin Keates / Natural
History Museum, London. 182 Dorling Kindersley: Ruth Jenkinson / Holts
Gems (crb, br). 184 Alamy Stock Photo: Alexey Kamenskiy (Sulfur B). 186
SuperStock: 3LH-Fine Art (crb/Stibnite B). 188 Getty Images / iStock:
petekarici (Marcasite B). 190 1stdibs.com: (bl/Chrysoberyl B). Alamy
Stock Photo: Halyna Kubei (crb/Chrysoberyl B). 192 Dorling Kindersley:
Holts Gems (crb/Diaspore B, bl/Diaspore B). 194 Dorling Kindersley:
Natural History Museum, London (Celestite B). 196 Dorling Kindersley:
Natural History Museum, London (crb/Aragonite B). 198 Dorling
Kindersley: Natural History Museum, London (crb/Anglesite B, bl/Anglesite
B). 200 Getty Images / iStock: VvoeVale (crb/Variscite B). 202 Bonhams
Auctioneers, London: (cr/Cordierite B). Dorling Kindersley: Holts Gems (br/
Cordierite B). 204 Bonhams Auctioneers, London: (cr/Chrysocolla B). 205
Dorling Kindersley: Natural History Museum, London (Zoisite). 206 Dorling
Kindersley: Holts Gems (br/Zoisite B); Natural History Museum, London
(cr/Zoisite B). 208 Dorling Kindersley: Holts Gems, Hatton Garden (br/
Olivine B); Holts Gems (bl/Olivine B). 210 Dorling Kindersley: Natural
History Museum, London (cr/Topaz B). Dreamstime.com: L Dreams (bl/
Topaz B). 211 Dorling Kindersley: Natural History Museum, London
(Sillimanite). 212 Dorling Kindersley: Natural History Museum, London (br/
Sillimanite B). 214 Dorling Kindersley: Natural History Museum, London
(crb/Turquoise B). 216 Dreamstime.com: Artshock (bl/Microcline B). 218
Dorling Kindersley: Natural History Museum, London (crb/Albite B, bl/
Albite B). 220 Alamy Stock Photo: Natural History Museum, London (bl/
Oligoclase B). Dorling Kindersley: Natural History Museum, London (br/
Oligoclase B). 222 Dorling Kindersley: Holts Gems (bl/Labradorite B). 224
Getty Images / iStock: chictype (bl/Talc B). 226 123RF.com: picsfive (bl/
Pyrophyllite B). Alamy Stock Photo: agefotostock / Historical Views (crb/
Pyrophyllite B). 227 Shutterstock.com: MarcelClemens (Rhodonite). 228
Bonhams Auctioneers, London: (crb/Rhodonite B, bl/Rhodonite B). 230
Alamy Stock Photo: De Agostini / Photo 1 / Universal Images Group North
America LLC (br/Axinite B). Dorling Kindersley: Natural History Museum,
London (cb/Axinite B). 232 Bonhams Auctioneers, London: (crb/Cyanite
B). 233 Alamy Stock Photo: PjrRocks (Chalcanthite). 234 Dorling
Kindersley: Natural History Museum, London (bl/Chalcanthite B, br/
Chalcanthite B). 236 Dorling Kindersley: Holts Gems (bl/Coral B); Natural
History Museum, London (br/Coral B). 238 Dreamstime.com: Valentyn75
(bl/Pearl B). 240 Mary Evans Picture Library: Alinari Archives, Florence -
Reproduced with the permission of Ministero per i beni e le attività culturali
(crb/Shell B). 241 Dreamstime.com: Cristian M. Vela (Amber). 242 Alamy
Stock Photo: Alexander Demianchuk / Reuters (br/Amber B). 244 Dorling
Kindersley: Holts Gems (crb/Copal B). 246 Getty Images: Ron Evans /
Photodisc (cl/Coal B). 250 Dorling Kindersley: Richard Leeney / Holts
Gems, Hatton Garden (b).

All other images © Dorling Kindersley